A WEE GUIDE TO
Flora
MacDonald

Flora mcdonald

A WEE GUIDE TO

Flora
MacDonald

David MacDonald

GOBLINSHEAD
Musselburgh

Wee Guide to Flora MacDonald

First Published 2003
Text © David MacDonald 2003
© Martin Coventry 2003

Published by GOBLINSHEAD
130B Inveresk Road
Musselburgh EH21 7AY Scotland
tel 0131 665 2894; *fax* 0131 653 6566
email goblinshead@sol.co.uk

British Library Cataloguing in Publication Data
A catalogue record for this book is available from the British
Library.

ISBN 1 899874 38 0

Typeset by GOBLINSHEAD using Desktop Publishing

If you would like a colour catalogue of our
publications please contact the publishers at
Goblinshead, 130B Inveresk Road,
Musselburgh EH21 7AY, Scotland, UK.

Look out for other related Goblinshead titles (available from
bookshops and other outlets, or directly from the publisher at
the address above):

Wee Guide to the Jacobites (£3.95)

Wee Guide to Rob Roy MacGregor (£3.95)

Contents

List of Illustrations

Foreword

Flora MacDonald was not a simple country girl, nor a Gaelic Joan of Arc – as she has been portrayed. Flora was an ordinary woman born into a prominent family of a prominent clan, with an extraordinary sense of courage and duty, which invoked both admiration and chivalry in all except the most despicable of men.

It is important in understanding Flora, and her clan the MacDonalds, to discuss briefly the historical, political and social background, particularly of her family. Flora's life spanned, and was intrinsically linked with, one of the most momentous periods of world history: the final eclipse of Scottish-Gaelic society, the beginning of the Highland and Island migration to North America, the failure of the Jacobite cause and any pretention the Stewarts had to ruling Britain, the foundation of modern parliamentary democracy, and the establishment of the United States of America.

D. MacD., Edinburgh, 2003

Acknowledgements

Particular thanks to Deborah Hunter at the National Gallery of Scotland; Barbara at Dunvegan Castle; Caroline Forsyth at Flodigarry Country House Hotel; Maggie Macdonald at Armadale Castle; Royal Hotel, Portree; Doug Houghton at Orkney Slide Library. Thanks also to Joyce Miller and Marion Pollock, and anyone I have forgotten.

Photos and maps by Martin Coventry, except –
Scottish National Portrait Gallery (SNPG): Flora MacDonald by unknown artist after Allan Ramsay (front cover); Flora MacDonald by Richard Wilson (frontispiece and page 34); Prince Charles Edward Stuart by Maurice Quentin de la Tour (page 10); Flora MacDonald by an unknown artist after Allan Ramsay (page 13); Prince Charles Edward Stuart (dressed as Betty Burke) by J. Williams (page 17); Prince Charles Edward Stuart – Reward for His Arrest by Cooper (page 19); Flora MacDonald by T. Faber after T. Hudson (page 30)
Eileen Barrie: Invergarry Castle (page 33)
Flodigarry Country House Hotel: Flora's cottage (page 41)
Dunvegan Castle: Relics of Flora, Dunvegan Castle (page 48)
David MacDonald: Flora's memorial at Kilmuir (page 50)
Doug Houghton: Flora's statue, Inverness Castle (page 53); Ruthven Barracks (page 83)

A WEE GUIDE TO

Flora
MacDonald

Calendar of Events

1722 Birth of Flora MacDonald at Milton, South Uist

1724 Death of Ranald, Flora's father

19 May 1745 Bonnie Prince Charlie raises Jacobite standard at Glenfinnan

16 April 1746 Battle of Culloden and defeat of Jacobites

20 June 1746 Flora agrees to help Charlie

21 June 1746 Flora apprehended at the ford

22 June 1746 Released by her stepfather and left for Nunton

23-27 June 1746 Preparation of Charlie's disguise

27 June 1746 Flora travels from Nunton to Rossinish

28 June 1746 Flora and Charlie sail to Skye, arrive at Monkstadt, then on to Kingsburgh House

29 June 1746 Flora parts from Charlie and leaves for Armadale with Neil

1-12 July 1746 Flora stays in Armadale

12 July 1746 Flora arrested and interrogated

July-November 1746 Flora is imprisoned in Dunstaffnage Castle, taken to Sleat on Skye, then Leith on board the *Bridgewater*. Flora transferred to the *Eltham*, the prison hulk the *Royal Sovereign*, then the Tower of London, before being lodged with Mr Dick

19 September 1746 Prince Charles leaves for France from Loch nan Uamh

23 November 1746 Death of Sir Alexander MacDonald of Sleat

4 July 1747 Jacobite prisoners freed; Flora freed a few days later

July 1747-April 1748 Flora in Edinburgh

19 April 1748 Flora shipwrecked returning to Skye

April-September 1748 Flora at Armadale

7 October 1748 Treaty of Aix-la-Chapelle: end of war between Britain and France

1748-1750 Flora in Edinburgh, York and London; interviewed by Forbes

July 1750 Flora returns to Skye

6 November 1750 Flora marries Allan MacDonald of Kingsburgh

1751 Flora and Allan move to Flodigarry

22 October 1751 Birth of son, Charles

18 February 1754 Birth of Anne

1755 Allan becomes factor of Trotternish

21 February 1755 Birth of Alexander

16 August 1756 Birth of Ranald

30 November 1757 Birth of James

March 1759 Flora, wife of Alexander MacDonald of Kingsburgh and Allan's mother, dies; Flora and family move back to Kingsburgh House

30 October 1759 Birth of John

1765 Cattle prices plummet; MacQueen fraud; Allan replaced as factor

1766 Sir James MacDonald of Sleat dies in Rome; new chief Sir Alexander

6 May 1766 Birth of Frances (Fanny); Flora is 44

1771 Black Spring

1771-1772 Great Hunger

13 February 1772 Alexander MacDonald of Kingsburgh, Allan's father, dies

1773 Dr Johnson and Boswell visit Flora and Allan at Kingsburgh House

1774 Flora and family sail to North Carolina

1774-1776 Plantation in Mount Vernon

27 February 1776 Battle of Moores Creek, heralding American War of Independence; Allan and Alexander captured

4 July 1776 Declaration of Independence signed

November 1777 Plantation confiscated by the Patriots

August 1777 Allan and Alexander freed

Late 1779 Flora returns to London because of poor health; learns of Alexander's death; falls ill

1780 Flora returns to Skye; learns of Ranald's death

1783 Allan's regiment disbanded: he retires on half pay

1784 Allan returns to Britain, first to London, then to Skye

1784-1787 Allan and Flora have no settled home

1787 Allan secures tack of Peinduin on Skye

4 March 1790 Death of Flora at Peinduin and she is buried at Kilmuir

20 September 1790 Death of Allan

Map 1: Flora's Scotland

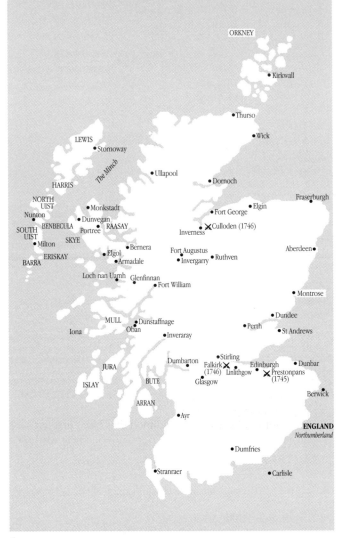

ORKNEY

•Kirkwall

•Thurso

•Wick

LEWIS
•Stornoway

The Minch

•Ullapool

HARRIS

•Dornoch

NORTH
UIST   Fraserburgh•
Nunton   •Monkstadt   •Elgin
              •Dunvegan   •Fort George
BENBECULA   Portree RAASAY
SOUTH   Inverness ✕Culloden (1746)
UIST   •Milton SKYE
ERISKAY   •Elgol   •Bernera   Aberdeen•
                •Armadale   Fort Augustus
BARRA   •Invergarry •Ruthven
        Loch nan Uamh •Glenfinnan
                    •Fort William
                                        •Montrose

                    MULL •Dunstaffnage   •Dundee
        Iona   Oban   •Perth •St Andrews
                    •Inveraray
        JURA   •Stirling
              Dumbarton• Falkirk✕ Edinburgh •Dunbar
                        (1746) Linlithgow ✕Prestonpans
        ISLAY   BUTE   (1745)
                    Glasgow•
                ARRAN   Berwick•

                    •Ayr
                                ENGLAND
                                Northumberland

                        •Dumfries
            •Stranraer   •Carlisle

1 – Flora and the MacDonalds

Flora was born at Milton on South Uist in 1722. Her father was Ranald MacDonald of Milton, of Clanranald, who died when she was two years old. Marion, her mother, the daughter of the celebrated Presbyterian minister Reverend MacDonald, subsequently married Hugh MacDonald of Armadale. Hugh MacDonald was from the Sleat branch of the clan and, although he had lost an eye, was an officer in the French army. He was reputed to be an excellent swordsman.

Although very little is known of Flora's early years, her education as a member of the Gaelic-speaking Highland gentry would have been to a similar standard as that of the English-speaking Lowland or British nobility. Since the *Bond and Statutes of Iona* in 1609, the sons of Gaelic gentlemen were required to be educated in the Lowlands. One of Flora's co-conspirators, Donald Roy MacDonald of Baleshare, used his time in hiding to write poetry in very good Latin, published in *Lyon in Mourning*. Sir Alexander MacDonald of Sleat, her stepfather's chief, completed his education at St Andrews University. This expensive education was not required for daughters, however, and Flora would have been educated locally at Nunton, the seat of her chief MacDonald of Clanranald.

Flora, who was a Presbyterian, would certainly have been able to read English sufficiently well to understand the Bible, which then was only available in English. Flora was reported by Dr Samuel Johnson to be 'uncommonly well-bred'. She was musical, an accomplishment which would have been expected in a lady of her day, indeed particularly so in the Gaelic world. Almost all activities were accompanied by song, such as waulking songs, songs for churning the milk, rowing boats, and so on. Poetry, which ranged from genealogy, sagas and romantic subjects, was also very popular in Highland areas.

It was not until late in her childhood that Flora first left Uist to visit both her mother Marion, who was now living at Armadale in Sleat on Skye, and her grandmother's folk at Largie in Kintyre. Her brother, Allan, was married with children and inherited the family home at Milton.

A brief overview of the clans, particularly with reference to the MacDonalds or Clan Donald, can help to understand Flora and her life and actions.

The MacDonalds, also known as 'the Great Clan', 'Headship of the Gael' or poetically 'Children of Conn of the Hundred Battles', were among the remnants of the once powerful peoples, now known as the Celts. In the first centuries BC, these peoples spread from the Ukraine to Spain; and as far south as Rome, which the Celtic Gauls sacked in 390 BC.

The MacDonalds were particularly proud of their ancestry. Although much of their blood was Norse, the heart through which it flowed was Gaelic. It was their Irish descent which they held most precious, claiming they came from the legendary 'Conn of the Hundred Battles', through the great Somerled, who established himself in the west and defeated the Vikings in the 12th century, and the Kings of Dalriada, who settled in Argyll from Ireland from the 6th century. The MacDonald Lords of the Isles, ruling from Finlaggan on Islay, were *de facto* sovereigns of western Scotland in the 15th century. The assistance given to the Irish by the MacDonalds against English invaders meant Irish genealogists also placed them among the principal Irish families. This proud lineage helped sustain the clan through many darker days.

The name MacDonald is commonly applied to all members of Clan Donald (Mac means son of), but some of the seven major

Finlaggan on Islay – power base of the MacDonald Lord of the Isles.

branches and over 300 families use other names: many are patronyms, such as MacIain, MacAlister and Martin. These were derived from the name, a particular attribute, or a characteristic of an important ancestor. The formal Gaelic name was in fact a recitation of the person's genealogy going back to Conn or Somerled. Much shorter names, for everyday usage, were based upon the person's father and tack. Flora was 'Flora, daughter of Ranald of Milton' or more simply 'Milton's daughter' as Ranald had only one daughter. Other MacDonald clansmen have names suggestive of other clans, such as MacLean and even Campbell, probably 'broken men', who had lost their clan or broken from it. These, particularly if they had been with a clan for a generation or more, would have been considered, and considered themselves, MacDonalds. In the 1745-6 Jacobite Rising, Campbells served in MacDonald regiments and, perhaps as a Clanranald clansman, in the Skye boat crew.

Kinship tied the chiefs and the people to each other in a father-child relationship: clan means children. As the father leads and protects his offspring, they in turn owe him obedience. It was not a blind obedience, however, and clansmen could and did refuse to follow their chief if they felt he was following the wrong cause. This is precisely what happened when Sir Alexander MacDonald of Sleat attempted to raise a Hanoverian battalion from Skye. Instead of the 1000 expected recruits, there were barely enough clansmen to man two companies: many, including Donald Roy MacDonald of Baleshare, defied their chief and joined the Jacobites. When the cause of chief and clansman coincided, the obedience of the clansman was unconditional. At the Battle of Culloden, a wounded Keppoch (another branch of the MacDonalds) clansman ordered his son to abandon him and assist their wounded chief, declaring that the son's duty to his chief was higher than that to his father.

Kinship could cross clan borders. At the Battle of Inverlochy in 1645, many Campbell lairds saved their lives by pleading kinship to the Campbell mothers, grandmothers, wives or aunts of the many MacDonald lairds. This kinship was more than sufficient to overcome the intentions of the MacDonalds to avenge the recent murders by the Campbells of MacDonald civilians in Scotland and Ireland.

The interclan kinship between Sir Alexander MacDonald of Sleat, whose mother was a MacLeod, as was Lady Clanranald, would confirm the peaceful co-existence and co-operation that marked MacDonald-MacLeod relations, especially on Skye. This interclan kinship could also have adverse consequences. It is likely that due to the close relationship between the MacLeods of Raasay and the MacDonnells of Glengarry (also MacDonalds), the MacLeods provided a Jacobite company which served in one of the battalions of the MacDonnells. This resulted in the savage second spoiling of Raasay by MacLeod militia from Skye, after the Campbells had been substantially responsible for the first rampage through the island.

In modern society people are more concerned with their rights, while in Flora's day most people would have been more aware of their obligations. The chief was himself obligated to hold land in trust for the clan, administering its best use, and organising its defence and justice.

There was a hierarchy of tenants, the most senior being the tacksmen, usually close relatives of the chief, who held leases (tacks) from the chief to sublet to farmer-warriors, who owed them rent and military service. The clan system had already survived the decline in clan warfare: the last MacDonald-MacLeod battle was in 1601. The fact that it may have been able to support perhaps as many as 40,000 people on Skye in 1745 illustrates its intrinsic viability, although it is true that many folk lived in poverty. Today Skye, which is one of the most prosperous parts of the Highlands, only supports 8,000 people.

It is easy to understand the affinity that could exist between Catholic MacDonalds and Catholic Stewarts, and also between the Stewarts and Episcopalians (Scottish Anglicans) who accepted the Stewarts' quasi-ordained status as the 'Lord's Anointed'. To the Presbyterians (Flora was brought up in the Presbyterian church), the Stewarts were their arch-enemies. It is particularly illustrative of the MacDonald's cohesiveness that the MacDonalds of Ardnamurchan (who were Presbyterian and had been under Campbell authority since their chiefs, the MacIains of Ardnamurchan, had been displaced early in the 17th century) joined the Jacobites in large numbers, forcing the few dozen Campbells and Hanoverians to seek refuge in Mingary Castle.

This broad spectrum support for the Stewarts from within Clan Donald was largely based upon a common ancestry. This is reflected in the earlier good relations between the Scottish kings and the Lords of the Isles, which was more of a fraternal alliance rather than a simple ruler-subject relationship. Envy of the increasing power and influence of the Lords, and the Stewarts' attempts to extend their power into the west, culminated in the destruction of the Lordship of the Isles by James IV in 1494, as well as plantations of Lowlanders and the ethnic cleansing of Gaels from some areas by James VI. After the execution of Charles I, the Stewart party sought to restore good relations with the powerful Highland clans, but they quickly forgot their erstwhile allies when Charles II regained the throne in 1660.

It is, therefore, surprising that the Gaels should have had anything to do with the Stewarts when James VII fled from Britain and from William of Orange. It was as much the massacre of the MacDonalds of Glencoe in 1692, sanctioned by William of Orange, and a coincidence of interests that committed many MacDonalds to the Jacobite cause – rather than any underlying love for the Stewarts. Perhaps an even more powerful inducement was 'The Prophecy', a messianic prediction that the Gaels would one day regain their former greatness in Scotland.

Sir Alexander MacDonald of Sleat, however, openly sided with the Hanoverians, although he probably had Jacobite sympathies. He most likely believed that the 1745 Jacobite Rising, led by Bonnie Prince Charlie, could only end in disaster. The outcome of a failed rebellion was crystal clear to Sir Alexander. His father had supported the failed Jacobite Rising of 1715-16 and had had his lands seized and forfeited. His clansmen were only able to buy back the estates and restore them to Sir Alexander in 1726. Failure would mean ruin.

Women warriors abound in Irish and Scottish Gaelic legend: Sgathach, a legendary female archer, had a school at Dun Sgathaich (the stronghold of Sgathach) in Sleat on Skye, which drew, among others, the legendary Ulster hero Cuchullin, after whom the nearby Cuillin mountains are called. Although women were finally excluded from any warrior role by the Law of the Innocents, there were some very active women in the politics of the time, particularly among the Jacobites. Many women had Jacobite sympathies even though their husbands were Hanoverian officers.

2 – *Bonnie Prince Charlie and Culloden*

When Prince Charles Edward Stewart (known to Jacobites as the 'Young Chevalier', the Hanoverians as the 'Young Pretender', and the general population as 'Bonnie Prince Charlie') had come to Scotland as the Regent of his father James VIII, France was already at war with Britain in the War of the Austrian Succession. Charles had finally landed in Moidart with only a few companions, instead of the promised French troops, arms and money. This had already caused the cautious Sir Alexander MacDonald of Sleat and MacLeod of MacLeod to advise him to return to France, and neither of them openly supported him.

Charlie refused to leave, and raised his father's standard on Clanranald territory, a branch of the MacDonalds, at Glenfinnan. After a whirlwind campaign, that took his mostly Highland army

Prince Charles Edward Stewart (Bonnie Prince Charlie) by Maurice Quentin de la Tour (SNPG).

deep into England, Prince Charles's forces conducted a successful retreat into Scotland. Then they were to suffer defeat at Culloden on Wednesday 16 April 1746 by a well-equipped Hanoverian army, which outnumbered the Jacobites by two-to-one.

The feared vicious aftermath now materialised. The Hanoverian commander-in-chief, William, Duke of Cumberland, the younger son of George I, ordered a root-and-branch extermination, not only of all fleeing rebels but anyone who gave them assistance. His treatment of prisoners earned him the epithet of 'Butcher'. The most barbarous treatment was reserved for the Gaels: the wounded were bayoneted where they lay. The French were taken into captivity and treated honourably.

The behaviour of the Hanoverian troops, sailors and marines, particularly those under Captains Scott and Ferguson, were particularly reprehensible. A favoured practice was raping of women, then leaving them naked after burning their homes, clothes and all sources of food. Mass rape on the Isle of Eigg was only thwarted because the women hid in a cave. After torture of their men did not reveal the hiding place, the would-be rapists consoled themselves by wantonly destroying their cattle.

Although the Campbell militia participated in the despoiling of the Highlands with great enthusiasm, there were exceptions. Campbell of Ardnamurchan successfully interceded on behalf of his MacDonald tenants. Major General John Campbell of Mamore, later 4th Duke of Argyll, who led the search for Prince Charles, was – by all accounts – a humane man.

Bonnie Prince Charlie certainly possessed some of the courage of his great-grandfather John III Sobieski, King of Poland, whose victorious record culminated as the 'Saviour of Vienna': John lifted the Turkish siege of Vienna in 1683.

Although generally of a cheerful disposition, Bonnie Prince Charlie was given to fits of melancholy, and even depression. Charles frequently behaved childishly and petulantly when he was not getting his own way. It was Charles who, over-ruling his experienced Scottish commanders, chose to fight at Culloden. His commanders believed that Culloden suited their enemy. The ground and the disposition of the army denied the Gael his preferred style of fighting, which was 'close-up and personal' in contrast to the 'shooting range' preferred by the British and other Europeans.

The MacDonalds were marshalled on the left wing, having been displaced from the right wing, the place of honour they had had since Bannockburn. This would have been a serious insult to their pride, but was the least of their concerns. Their position, on the left, was not only twice the distance from the enemy as the rest of the Jacobite army, but their exposed flank was threatened by almost all of the enemy cavalry; they also faced half of its infantry and many cannon, which were already tearing gaps in their ranks with round-shot. They charged, following MacDonald of Keppoch's lead, but nearly half of them were mown down by a heavy fire of grape-shot and massed musketry. The MacDonalds retreated. The collapse of the right wing of the Jacobite army forced a general rout.

At least 4000 men not only escaped but reformed at Ruthven Barracks, near Kingussie, with the intention to continue the rising. This was in part thanks to those units which fought on covering the retreat: Colonel Jean MacDonnell, a French-Scot, charged his 60 horsemen into the teeth of the pursuing 500 dragoons. The 4000 survivors of the battle were dismayed when Charles, who had fled west, declined to continue the fight, and declared that he would return to France as soon as possible.

Monument to the Highlanders who fought and died for the Jacobites at the Battle of Culloden in 1746.

3 – Flora and Charlie

During the summer, it was usual to take the black cattle, on which much of the economy of Scotland depended, to the shielings, the higher pastures, now free of snow, to graze. This had the

Flora MacDonald – her portrait and signature (by an unknown artist after Allan Ramsay (SNPG)).

advantage of allowing the lower land, most suitable for arable farming, to be used for oats, wheat and other crops. Looking after the cattle in the shieling was generally women's work. During the night of Saturday 20 June 1746, Flora, who was about 24 years of age, was wakened from sleep by Neil MacDonald at the shieling at Alisary in South Uist.

He asked her to help Prince Charles Edward Stewart, the Young Chevalier.

This was to be the first time Flora was to meet the Prince, who was wearing Highland dress, presumably the famous 'Lady MacDonald of Borodale's Gift' or the 'Jacobite' tartan.

Map 2: The Western Isles

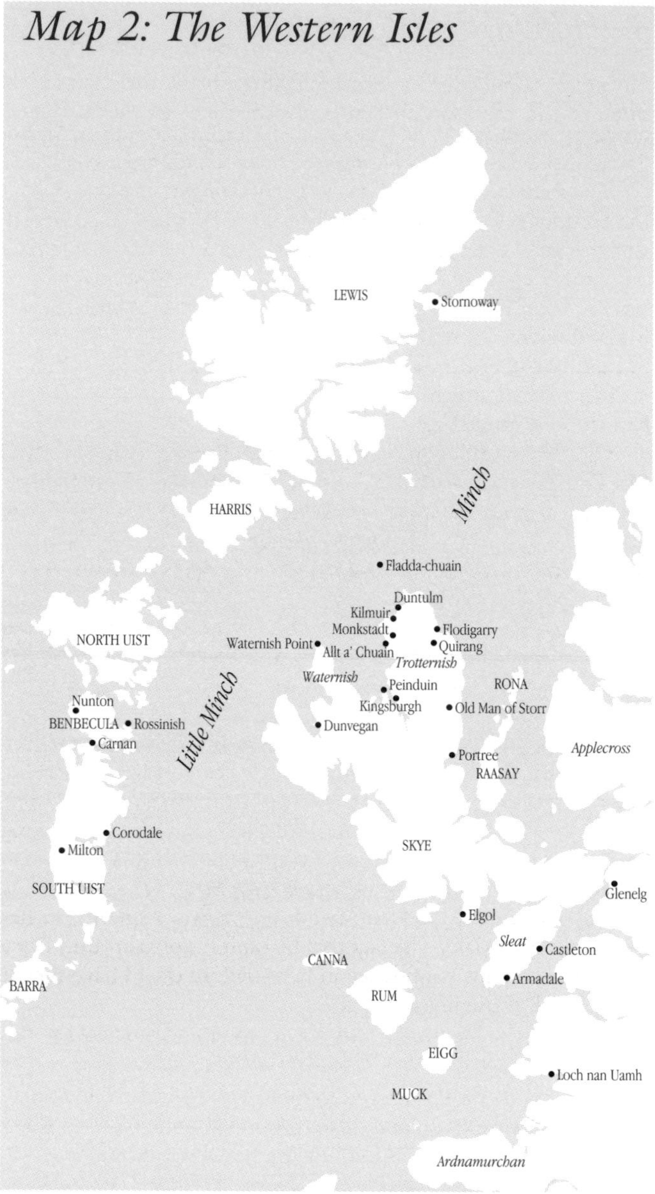

LEWIS

● Stornoway

Minch

HARRIS

● Fladda-chuain

Duntulm

Kilmuir

Monkstadt

● Flodigarry

NORTH UIST

Waternish Point ● Allt a' Chuain ● Quirang

Trotternish

Waternish ● Peinduin

Nunton

RONA

BENBECULA ● Rossinish

Kingsburgh ● Old Man of Storr

● Carnan

● Dunvegan

Little Minch

Applecross

● Portree

RAASAY

● Corodale

● Milton

SKYE

SOUTH UIST

Glenelg

● Elgol

Sleat ● Castleton

CANNA

● Armadale

BARRA

RUM

EIGG

● Loch nan Uamh

MUCK

Ardnamurchan

The Prince had already been a fugitive for several weeks. He had been taken to Uist so that he would best be able to get a ship back to France. Alexander MacDonald of Boisdale provided him with shelter and sustenance in Corodale. Hanoverian forces, however, were hot on his heels as, under interrogation, Simon Fraser, Lord Lovat, had betrayed Charlie's hiding place of Uist.

The ships of the Royal Navy were patrolling the waters around the Hebrides. On 15 June, MacDonald of Boisdale was arrested, and soldiers under the brutal Captain Scott had already landed on South Uist from Barra, and had tortured Lady MacDonald of Boisdale and her household to reveal the Prince's whereabouts. Major General John Campbell of Mamore, responsible for trying to capture the Prince, was moving south towards Scott, who was in turn moving north. Time was running out for the Prince: he had to been moved off Uist.

Charles was accompanied by two French officers: Neil MacDonald, a native of Uist, born in 1719 and son of MacEachen, the tacksman of Howbeg; and Felix O'Neille, an Italian of Irish descent, who had previously served in the Spanish army. Neil had been brought to Paris by Aeneas MacDonald, the Parisian banker with whom Charles had lodged prior to setting out for Scotland. Neil trained for the priesthood, but prior to ordination was commissioned into the French army. In addition to being a Gaelic speaker, he knew both the families and geography of Uist.

Charles had been referred to Flora by her stepfather, Hugh MacDonald of Armadale, who was supposed to be directing the hunt for the Prince. He wanted Charles to be moved to Skye, where, according to Neil's recall 'he was sure to be protected by Lady Margaret MacDonald' (wife of Sir Alexander MacDonald of Sleat). But why involve his stepdaughter Flora in such a dangerous venture? Hugh planned that Flora should take the Prince, disguised as her Irish maid, to Skye as a spinner to her mother in Armadale. The fact that he built his plan around Flora would indicate his confidence in her – failure could have meant death for all those involved.

Why did the MacDonalds continue to give so much assistance to Charles and suffer the devastation of their lands and clan by the Hanoverians? Perhaps the sensible thing would have been to hand the Prince over, not only ingratiating themselves with the Hanoverians, who would have called off their punitive search, but also receiving a bounty of £30,000, a considerable sum in those days.

In spite of their Lowland education and difference in religious and political beliefs, most MacDonald gentry were still Gaels at heart, holding their prized Highland virtues, of which hospitality, accompanied by an obligation of protection, were among the highest. It was upon MacDonald land that Charles had landed, raised his standard, and to which he had now fled. It would have been to Clan Donald's eternal shame if Charles had been captured or come to harm on its land. Flora would instinctively have understood this and quickly acquiesced to her stepfather's plan. She did have well-warranted doubts that Bonnie Prince Charlie could carry out the role required of him – and she was unwilling to contribute to the ruin of her chief MacDonald of Clanranald.

Flora set out for Lady Clanranald's house at Nunton on Benbecula, while Charles set off for the Corodale mountains with Neil and O'Neille. Flora now knew that Charles's safety rested upon her alone.

Flora was intercepted by Skye militia as she crossed to Benbecula by the ford of Gregory. She was held overnight and then taken to their officer in the morning.

Meanwhile, immediately upon reaching Corodale, the impatient Prince sent Neil MacDonald off to Nunton to find out how the plan was progressing. When Neil reached Carnan, he found out that not only was the tide in but that he was surrounded by soldiers, who kept him overnight on the South Uist side of the ford, before taking him across at dawn.

When he was taken before the commanding officer, Neil found him having breakfast with Flora. Luckily, the officer was none other than Flora's stepfather Hugh MacDonald of Armadale, who ordered that he was to be released. Flora then continued her journey to Nunton, whereas Neil was instructed to move Charles across the strait to Rossinish on Benbecula and to await her there. It would appear that Hugh provided Flora with a passport for herself, Neil and a Betty Burke in an open letter addressed to his wife and dated 22 June. In it he explained that the presence of so many soldiers was frightening Flora, so he was sending her to join her mother in Armadale on Skye. Betty Burke, an Irish spinner of fine lint and wool, was accompanying Flora, as he believed that she would be useful. Both were in care of Neil MacDonald, a servant.

Armadale was across the Sound of Sleat from the extensive Clanranald mainland, where the Prince could best hide until rescued by ship. This long journey necessitated the use of the disguise of Betty Burke as the Prince passed through Skye.

It took them nearly five days to prepare the disguise because Charles was a tall man for his day and woman's clothes of the right size would not readily be available. The gown was made of calico with a floral pattern, and was accompanied by a mantle made after the Irish fashion, with a large hood, a cap, and a broad apron. Shoes and stockings were also provided. The time spent making Betty Burke's clothes would appear to have been worthwhile. Although Charles's entirely inappropriate conduct drew attention to Betty Burke, no comment made suggested that Betty was actually a man in drag.

Bonnie Prince Charlie dressed as Betty Burke
(by J. Williams (SNPG)).

Why was Charles disguised as woman? There were a number of reasons. To escape to Skye would mean the real risk of meeting Hanoverian troops to whom details of his description would have been widely distributed. His foreign mannerisms and accent would quickly betray him if he continued to wear Highland dress, as happened later in MacNab's Inn. It is clear from the many portraits of Charles that he had very fine, almost feminine features, and a slim, if not slight, frame. The specific disguise as an Irish woman could be used to explain away his height and behaviour. The painting by J. Williams (previous page) gives an idea of what Charles looked like as Betty Burke, although in a different dress.

Although Charles spoke some Gaelic (having had a Gaelic tutor, the famous Gaelic poet Captain Alasdair MacMhaighster, assigned to him) neither the Prince's accent nor dialect would have been right for Skye. But since he was travelling as a lady's maid, questions would be directed to Flora, the lady, rather than to the subordinate maid. If he had accompanied Flora as a man, especially someone with an air of authority, questions would have been addressed to him. To further protect Charles and Flora, the passport included Neil, who would have a Uist accent and therefore was a convincing companion.

While all these preparations were being made, Hugh MacDonald was directing Major General John Campbell of Mamore away from Charles. On 27 June, Neil had been sent to hurry up the preparation of the dress as Lieutenant John MacDonald, a militia officer, had told Charles a suitable boat was ready. Late that evening, Flora travelled to Rossinish in the company of her brother Angus of Milton, Neil, and Lady Clanranald.

Just when they settled down for a simple meal, a herd-boy ran in to warn them that Major General Campbell had landed with a strong force just three miles away. Fearing that they had been betrayed, Flora, the Prince, Neil and their crew immediately took to the sea and fled.

On the morning of 28 June, a messenger from Nunton informed them that Campbell and Ferguson had reached Nunton at 8.00 that morning, and demanded that Lady Clanranald should return by 12.00 – with the threat that her household would suffer. Upon hearing this, Lady Clanranald and her daughter returned to Nunton, there telling Major General Campbell that she had been attending to a sick child. She was arrested, with her husband, a few days later and sent to London.

Assembled with Flora were the boat's crew, most of them MacDonalds, a son of the Clanranald gentry, some off-duty Sleat militia, and two clansmen, as well as the pilot Donald MacLeod of Galtrigal. Charles had become very difficult, first insisting that if O'Neille did not go then he would not go either, even suggesting that O'Neille should use Neil's passport. Flora firmly refused.

Once all those not travelling to Skye had left, Flora revealed Charles's disguise. The Prince took an immediate dislike to the head-dress, but Flora insisted that he should wear it as it had been specially designed to conceal as much of his face as possible.

Neil MacDonald was appalled how poorly Charles adjusted to his role as Betty Burke. Furthermore, Charles demanded to be allowed to conceal a pistol about his person. This request was flatly refused, although he was allowed a short heavy cudgel.

Bonnie Prince Charlie – Reward for His Arrest (by Cooper (SNPG)).

4 – 'Over the Sea to Skye'

The Minch was patrolled by the Royal Navy, as it was clear that flight back to Skye was the only escape route. The Hanoverians thought that they were making for Fladda-chuain, an island to the north of Skye in the middle of the Minch, which could be a staging post for a further flight back to the Jacobite territory on the mainland. Land could also be made at Elgol on the south of Skye. This was MacKinnon land: the MacKinnons were the only clan on Skye who unreservedly joined Charles and the Rising – they served in the Keppoch regiment. As both destinations would have made sense, the Hanoverians, it was hoped, would be too busy looking north and south, and would be less likely to notice the Prince slipping into Skye directly from the west.

The craft used was a standard eight-oared fishing boat, and had been borrowed by Aeneas MacDonald, who was responsible for the army's paychest. The low profile of such a craft would have made it difficult to see at sea, and meant it would be easier to hide. The night of the voyage, Saturday 28 June, was clear, hardly ideal for an unobserved crossing. Just when they were about to put to sea, boats full of Hanoverian troops sailed near them, forcing Flora and her companions to lie low until they passed. The second attempt, however, was successful and they crossed the Little Minch.

As they neared the Waternish Peninsula on Skye, a freshening westerly wind developed and heavy rain began to fall. Thick fog robbed them of sight of land. Charles sang several songs from the 1715 Rising, and seemed to be in good spirits. They then found themselves too close to the shore, and had to make their way up the coast to Waternish Point. Before rounding the point, they landed because the crew were exhausted. They ate bread and butter, and drank water that fell from a rock, then rested for an hour before putting back out to sea.

When they rounded Waternish Point, they were challenged by MacLeod militia, who fired upon them.

Flora and her companions made land at Allt na Chuain, just south of Monkstadt, Sir Alexander MacDonald of Sleat's home, on Trotternish. Although a small haven, it was normally guarded. Because it was now Sunday, however, the commander, Lieutenant MacLeod, had gone to church, taking his men with him.

Monkstadt House, now a ruin – Flora came here after bringing Bonnie Prince Charlie from Benbecula across to Skye.

Although Sir Alexander MacDonald of Sleat was a senior Hanoverian officer, his wife Lady Margaret was an enthusiastic Jacobite, who had sent gifts and shirts to Charles when he was at Corodale. Charles was left with the crew while Flora and Neil went to Monkstadt to make further arrangements with Lady Margaret for Charles's flight through Skye.

Although Lady Margaret knew that Charles was on his way to her, she did not know when he would arrive, until told so by the wife of MacDonald of Kirkibost (who was a Hanoverian officer), who had arrived the previous day. While at Monkstadt, Flora was questioned by Lieutenant MacLeod, a subordinate of Major MacLeod of Talisker, about the location of her boat and travelling companions. MacLeod, although having a reputation for diligence, on this occasion did nothing further. Flora kept him engaged in small talk to prevent him seeking out the boat or Lady Margaret, who was still trying to extricate her family from a dangerous, even life-threatening, situation. If Charles was captured so close to her home, Sir Alexander would be ruined.

Alexander MacDonald of Kingsburgh (whose son Allan Flora eventually married), Sir Alexander's chamberlain or factor (estate manager), had been released from his commission in the militia the previous week. He advised Lady Margaret not to bring Charles into her home. MacDonald of Kirkibost's wife had been temporarily apprehended the previous day by the same MacLeod militia who had fired on Flora's boat. It appeared that word had leaked out that it was proposed to smuggle Charles to Skye disguised as a woman. A new plan had to be made.

MacDonald of Kingsburgh sent for Donald Roy MacDonald of Baleshare, who had been wounded in the foot at Culloden. Donald Roy had been able to hirple from the battlefield and fled back to Skye, where he was treated by Dr MacLean, Sir Alexander's own physician. When Donald Roy learned of Lady Margaret's plight, he borrowed Dr MacLean's horse and rode to Monkstadt, where he saw both MacDonald of Kingsburgh and Lady Margaret still speaking in the garden. Following a discussion, during which a new plan was laid, he left to find MacLeod of Rona, who was hiding on Sleat land, to arrange the next step in Charles's escape.

It was decided that Neil should go back and move Charles away from the small haven as Lieutenant MacLeod's guard was soon to return. MacDonald of Kingsburgh, rather than Flora, would go to retrieve Charles and conduct him to Kingsburgh House. Hugh's passport and Flora's continued role in the new escape plan were no longer needed – indeed, the continued existence of the passport could incriminate her and Hugh. The passport should have been destroyed immediately, but the most serious mistake was to send the boat and crew back to Uist.

Flora went to Kingsburgh House in the company of MacDonald of Kirkibost's wife and her daughter. Flora left Monkstadt in the evening, an hour after sunset, but as she journeyed south, she encountered several groups of people coming back from church, who were discussing the bizarre Irish woman, undoubtedly Betty Burke, whom they had met on the road.

The disguised Prince's behaviour was noticeable, even in the twilight. Betty Burke had a manly stride and spoke to MacDonald of Kingsburgh, who was a factor and an important individual, as an equal rather than as a maid might. Betty had also hauled her petticoats to an indecent height while crossing a stream.

MacDonald of Kingsburgh quickly realised that the Prince was attracting too much attention, feared meeting local Hanoverian militia, and led Charles by a lesser-used track closer to the coast.

Both parties arrived at Kingsburgh House late in the evening at about the same time. Alexander MacDonald of Kingsburgh announced his guests as friends of 'Milton's daughter', thus reducing their status in the eyes of the servants, who would have paid them less attention. The Prince was smuggled into the house.

The behaviour of Betty Burke drew the attention of MacDonald of Kingsburgh's wife, who was also called Flora, and her daughter Anne, wife of MacAlistair of Skirinish (a militia officer). Alexander quickly took Charles into the parlour. There the Prince, still dressed as Betty Burke, greeted Kingsburgh's wife with a salute and kissed her hand: this could have left little doubt in her mind that this was a man. When her husband confirmed that it was Prince Charles Edward Stewart, she recoiled in fear, saying that they would all hang. Alexander replied that since one can only die once, giving succour to Charles was a good thing to die for.

His wife served supper herself in order to hide their guest's identity from their servants. Supper consisted of eggs, sliced meat, bread and good English beer. Alexander, Neil and Charles were left alone to drink, then the Prince had a bath and retired. He was awoken at noon the next day to find that Flora and Neil had already left for Portree by the main road.

Charles allowed Anne MacAlistair to cut a lock of his hair, which she then gave to her mother, who in turn gave half of it to Flora when she married Allan, her son. She also put away both bed sheets: one was buried with her, the other was later passed to Flora.

The Prince left Kingsburgh House still disguised as Betty Burke, so as not to raise suspicion among the servants who had seen him arrive. Later, in a wood a mile from Kingsburgh, he changed into clothes that belonged to Anne MacAlistair's husband. Most of his disguise as Betty Burke – including the incriminating Irish-style cloak, hood and cap – was burnt, but the apron and garters were eventually conveyed to Flora – and the dress was made into a bedspread.

Once the Prince had changed, he was guided by MacQueen, MacDonald of Kingsburgh's herd boy, by a back route to Portree. They were drenched by heavy rain. When they reached Portree, the Prince hid while MacQueen fetched Donald Roy, who then brought them into MacNab's Inn. The inn, owned by Charles MacNab, was the largest house in the town, and on the site of which now stands the Royal Hotel. There Charles found Flora and Neil. After a meal, Neil left with Charles to take him to

MacLeod of Raasay, who was to ferry the Prince to the island at this point. Bonnie Prince Charlie may have given Flora a locket, made of gold, with his portrait when they parted, although one of her daughters said he only gave Flora some coins.

Flora and Charles were not to meet again, but the part she had played in ferrying him from Uist to Skye would have long-lasting consequences for her.

MacLeod had to drag a boat from the fish pools in Loch Leitham, below the Old Man of Storr, down to the shore, then to get over to Raasay to get a larger boat which had been overlooked by the rampaging Hanoverians. After Charles and Neil left, MacNab confided to Flora that he suspected the tall, distinguished gentleman accompanying them was none other than Bonnie Prince Charlie.

Charles was eventually moved back to Clanranald territory, where he was kept in hiding by the MacDonalds until a French ship picked him up from Loch nam Uamh on 19 September.

Charles returned safely to France, but never again set foot in Scotland.

Meanwhile Captain Ferguson was on his way to Skye in the *Furnace*. Following the arrest of Flora's boat crew on their return to Uist, the Hanoverians knew that Charles had fled to Skye. They went to Monkstadt and first interviewed Lady Margaret MacDonald, who by now had regained her composure. She lied with sufficient conviction to satisfy Campbell and Ferguson that she had had nothing to do with the fugitive Prince.

Campbell and Ferguson proceeded to Kingsburgh House, but decided to employ subterfuge. They lured a maid from the house back to their ship and persuaded her to talk. It became clear that the servants thought that the guest at Kingsburgh House had been none other than the Bonnie Prince.

When Ferguson, who had a reputation for brutality, returned to Kingsburgh, he was taken aback by the dryness and bluntness of the lady of the house's reception. She said to him: 'If Ferguson is to be our judge then God help us!'. To this he lamely tried to explain that he had been miscalled.

He was shown the rooms that Flora and Betty Burke, supposedly her maid, had been given. He remarked that Betty had a decidedly better room that her mistress Flora. Alexander

MacDonald of Kingsburgh and his daughter Anne were arrested. MacDonald was sent to Inverness, where his chief, Sir Alexander MacDonald of Sleat, was stationed, and was nominally placed into his custody. While there, he was released 'in error', but Sir Alexander, who would have been formally informed of his release, immediately took him to the Duke of Cumberland, who was about to proclaim MacDonald of Kingsburgh an escaped prisoner and fugitive. There was a rather sharp exchange of words between Cumberland and Sir Alexander. It is possible that the 'error' in releasing MacDonald of Kingsburgh was an attempt to discredit Sir Alexander himself, whom Cumberland had earlier denounced as 'the great rebel'. Alexander MacDonald of Kingsburgh was eventually sent to Edinburgh Castle, where 'he spent a year in prison as the price of one night's lodging'.

Old Man of Storr – Bonnie Prince Charlie was ferried across to Raasay with a boat from Loch Leitham.

5 – *Honourable Captivity*

Accompanied by Neil, Flora reached Armadale on 1 July. On 12 July she was informed that she was to be interviewed by Roderick MacDonald, a lawyer acting for Major John MacLeod of Talisker, at Castleton, some four miles away. Before leaving Armadale, Donald Roy claimed that this was a trap, persuaded her to give him Hugh's letter, which he told her he would destroy along with other incriminating documents.

She was intercepted on her way to Castleton, arrested by Captain Ferguson. The circumstances of her arrest suggest the Skye militia colluded with Ferguson, undoubtedly to avoid a confrontation at Armadale. Flora was taken to Applecross Bay, where Major General Campbell was waiting to interview her.

She took full responsibility for smuggling Charles to Skye, but she protected Lady Margaret, and thereby Sir Alexander, Hugh MacDonald of Armadale, Alexander MacDonald of Kingsburgh, Donald Roy and Lieutenant MacLeod, among many others. She insisted that Lieutenant MacLeod did not come down to Allt na Chuain and had not searched the boat. Although Major General Campbell knew she was lying to protect her co-conspirators, he was impressed by her calm and clear answers.

The central role of Flora in Prince Charles's escape required that she be sent for trial: she was the last of the 26 prisoners being sent to London, almost all of them associated with Charles's time as a fugitive. Others included Lady Clanranald, MacDonald of Boisdale, Donald MacLeod of Galtrigal, Neil's brother Angus, and some of the boatmen who ferried Charles to Skye. Major General Campbell ignored Cumberland's orders for torture, and instead ordered that Flora be treated with the greatest respect.

Campbell must have believed that there was a mastermind, an individual with sufficient influence and ability to direct Charles's escape, perhaps assisted by a few others, allowing the Prince to evade the many troops and ships dedicated to his capture. At one time, the Royal Navy was diverted to St Kilda, and often the substantial land forces would be in the wrong place at the wrong time. Although there appeared to be a constant leak of information to Hanoverian spies, every time it was thought that they were about to capture Charles, he would escape. It was the identity of this supposed mastermind that Campbell needed.

It would appear that Major General Campbell was suspicious of Hugh MacDonald, but had no real evidence. Hugh, aware that he could be arrested, remained at large on Skye, where he was not only feared and respected, but it was also one of the few places that was more or less off limits to marauding Hanoverians. This was due to Sir Alexander's influence at the Duke of Cumberland's headquarters, and possibly the presence of MacDonald and MacLeod militia at all ports.

Sir Alexander MacDonald of Sleat tried hard to secure his factor Alexander MacDonald of Kingsburgh's freedom. He was assisted in this by his wife, Lady Margaret, but she put the blame for the whole affair on Flora, referring to her as that 'foolish girl' and 'gypsy' who 'intruded the disturber to the kingdom' (Charles) into Kingsburgh House. These representations did not achieve MacDonald of Kingsburgh's freedom. Margaret's resentment of Flora became even more vitriolic after Sir Alexander died of pleurisy on his way to London to appeal on MacDonald of Kingsburgh's behalf.

Flora was transferred to the *Eltham* under the command of the polite and generous Commodore Thomas Smith, normally a very stern man, who had overall command of all Royal Naval forces in western Scotland. He arranged for Flora to visit her mother in Sleat for a few hours in order to say goodbye. He

Dunstaffnage Castle – Flora was imprisoned here for a few days before being taken south.

allowed Flora to bring Kate MacDonald, who offered to run all risks with Flora. Flora was then taken to Dunstaffnage Castle, where she was confined for a few days, before being sent on the *Eltham* to Leith. During the voyage, Commodore Smith was like a father to Flora, cautioning to keep her to her story when she was subsequently questioned.

She was transferred to the *Bridgewater*, which was commanded by Captain Knowler, who also treated her with the utmost decency and politeness. While on board, she was visited by well wishers from many walks of life, as well as Jacobite groupies, or the merely curious, who wanted to be in proximity of the woman who was in the company of Bonnie Prince Charlie. They subjected her to what must have seemed to her, as a Highland woman, very strange requests. This included resting their heads in her lap because Charles, when sleeping, had rested his there during the boat trip across to Skye.

Other visitors took the opportunity to turn their visit into a dance, although Flora refused to take part, saying that she could not dance until she knew that Charles was safe. In reality, she was aware of her plight, and the ongoing trials and executions, and would not have been particularly disposed to dancing. More practically, Mrs Ferguson of Pitfour gave her a Bible because Flora had only a prayer book, and Lady Bruce provided her with linen, thread and needle to give her something to do to pass the time. On 7 November, her 'honourable captivity' was transferred back to the *Eltham* and she was conveyed to London as a prisoner of state.

On 18 November, on arrival at the Nore, she was transferred to the *Royal Sovereign*, a disease-ridden prison ship, but only for a few days. From here, she was taken to the Tower of London, but again her stay was brief. Both Commodore Smith and Major General Campbell prevailed upon Lord Albemarle, who had replaced the Duke of Cumberland as Commander-in-Chief in Scotland, to ensure that she was lodged in a messenger home, rather than a prison. The captains with whom she had been imprisoned added their support.

She was placed under house arrest at the home of Mr William Dick, which was considered to be the best of the messenger houses in which high-ranking prisoners were kept. She was visited by George, Prince of Wales and heir to the British throne. This visit might well have been motivated by George's strong dislike of his younger brother, the Duke of Cumberland, in addition to honouring a courageous and gallant foe in Flora.

George asked why she had helped Prince Charles, and she (wisely perhaps) responded that she felt she could not but assist any creature in trouble and that if he, the Prince of Wales, was in such trouble she would similarly assist him.

She was soon joined by other Jacobite prisoners, including Aeneas MacDonald. Although they were confined in a cold attic, they were allowed out of the house provided they remained in the company of one of Mr Dick's daughters. Nevertheless, the congeniality of the group could not offset the constant fear with continuing trials and executions in London and elsewhere: this would have been heightened when Aeneas was taken and confined in Newgate Prison.

Although 120 men were executed after a trial, many more had been summarily slain upon capture or had died under torture. A number of the Scottish gentry were condemned to death and executed in public at the Tower Hill in London. One such public spectacle, the execution of Simon Fraser, Lord Lovat, drew such enormous crowds that wooden stands had been constructed. One collapsed, killing 50 spectators, and Fraser is said to have remarked: 'the more mischief, the better sport'.

London society's response to Flora was entirely different, not only because she was a young woman, about whom most favourable reports were circulating, but also because of a charm offensive. Two pamphlets were released: *Alexis*, an anonymous parody of the recently failed Rising, and the second by Drummond, a loyal Hanoverian, which exonerated Flora.

These reports and pamphlets, in conjunction with the executions, helped assuage the anti-Jacobite feelings in London. The Duke of Cumberland, who was once feted by London society ladies wearing the Sweet William rose in his honour, was now vilified as the details of his conduct in the aftermath of Culloden became widely known. Once again, ladies in London and Edinburgh sported newly fashioned tartan dresses, garnished with the white Jacobite cockade. In Edinburgh they even marched in procession to visit friends imprisoned in Edinburgh Castle.

In Flora's day, a well-born lady's greatest, if not sole, social function was to produce an heir, and if possible a spare son and a couple of daughters. When not required by her husband, she would be left to her religious devotions and the distractions of the drawing room. It was particularly remarkable, therefore, to see women at the forefront of the Jacobite cause, even after it was lost. While around two thirds of men in Edinburgh were Hanoverian, almost all the women were for the Jacobites. This was not just confined to Britain. Louis XV of France made himself unpopular, even with his own family, when he had Bonnie Prince Charlie thrown out of France. Although many husbands and fathers would try to ascribe this malady in their womenfolk to 'the feebleness of the female mind', the women had become aware of their own political influence.

Flora MacDonald (by T. Faber after T. Hudson (SNPG)).

6 – *Freedom*

When the Act of Indemnity was passed by Parliament in 1747, most Jacobite prisoners were released. Flora, however, was not given her freedom until a couple of days later – the reason is not known. Of the 21 ladies of rank who were imprisoned, only one was transported, whereas 22 of the 56 ordinary women, mainly wives of ordinary soldiers, were banished. Of the 3471 taken prisoner, about one quarter were transported, 3% were executed, and one sixth died in captivity from starvation, disease or abuse. Aeneas MacDonald was expressly exempt from the Act of Indemnity, and was eventually condemned to death. The death penalty was set aside because he was considered to be more of a citizen of France than Britain – he was then exiled.

Flora did not immediately return to Skye as might have been expected. She lodged with Lady Primrose, and had at least one portrait painted. Funds raised for Flora by Lady Primrose finally amounted to £1500. Flora travelled to Edinburgh, but, because she was famous, took an assumed name, Miss Robertson. She was accompanied by Captain MacLeod of Raasay, travelling as Mr Robertson, her brother.

Once in Edinburgh she attended Mr David Beatt's school to improve her writing. The diligence she applied to her studies clearly bore fruit: her letters were clear, concise and attractive in comparison to the ponderous prose produced by many of her contemporaries. Her writing betrayed a neat orderly mind.

Her decision to remain in Edinburgh, away from her family, could not have only been to improve her writing, or even receive the adulation of an admiring public – because she was almost a recluse. The principle reason may have been that folk in Skye thought she had got off lightly when many innocent people suffered death or loss of property and, even more, she had also benefited financially. Her arch-enemy was Lady Margaret, who blamed her for the death of her husband, Sir Alexander.

While in Edinburgh, she was interviewed on three occasions by Bishop Forbes, who like many Episcopal clergy was a Jacobite and had been imprisoned. His collection of documents and interviews was subsequently published in three volumes as *Lyon in Mourning* by the Scottish Historical Society. During these interviews, Flora was still careful to protect Hugh MacDonald, but she now saw no need to hide the involvement of Lady Margaret.

Forbes seems to have had something of an obsession with the letter/passport Hugh had written for the historic journey that June night in 1746. He was not content with the straightforward facts that had appeared to satisfy Major General Campbell. From the correspondence he included in *Lyon in Mourning*, he had enlisted the chief of MacLeod in his efforts to uncover the original document, which may not have been destroyed at Armadale and was still in the possession of Alexander MacDonald of Kingsburgh. MacDonald never let anyone read it and, when pressed by MacLeod, released a copy, with the caveat that it was not an actual copy but an edition of the letter. Flora and her co-conspirators were sensible to maintain secrecy over the exact wording of the passport as in 1752 a Dr Cameron was executed on a treason charge dating from the Jacobite Rising of 1745-6. Hugh would have remained at risk because he had never been captured in 1746 and would likely not have benefited from the Act of Indemnity. It is likely that if the document had survived, it was then destroyed. Although MacDonald of Kingsburgh's edited copy (or a copy of it) was in the possession of one of Flora's granddaughters in the early 19th century, no further mention is made of Hugh's letter.

On 19 April 1748 Flora was shipwrecked while travelling back to Skye, and she would have drowned had she not been saved by an unnamed Highlander. She stayed with her mother at Armadale until September, then returned to Edinburgh, journeyed to York for a few days, and then returned to London, where she stayed until 1749. More portraits were painted, including one that year by Allan Ramsay. She returned to Edinburgh for another interview with Bishop Forbes on 11 July, before going back to Skye.

By then the Jacobite cause was finished. On 7 October 1748 the Treaty of Aix-la-Chapelle, which ended the War of the Austrian Succession, had been signed between France and Britain, requiring France to expel all Jacobites. Bonnie Prince Charlie had to leave France, although he was given a generous pension. Charles refused and eventually was arrested, imprisoned and deported in early 1749. This effectively ended the Jacobite cause, and any ambitions the Stewarts had of recovering the throne were further confounded when the Pope refused to recognise Charles's claim after the death of his father James on 1 January 1766.

The Highlands to which Flora returned had been utterly transformed. The military power of the clans and the power of their chiefs was destroyed in the Disarming Act of 1746, with the prohibition of the keeping, owning or carrying of weapons; and the abolition of heritable jurisdictions in 1747. The Disarming Act was not entirely successful, and duelling continued: one of Flora's grandsons (son of her daughter Anne) was killed by a MacDonnell of Glengarry in a duel. Nor did it stop clan-related attacks. The Act of Annexation, which confiscated the estates of some 14 clans, resulted in violence when the tenants rejected their new landlords. The 'Red Fox', Colin Campbell of Glenure, the new factor of the confiscated Stewart of Appin estate, was shot and killed in 1752 while on his way to evict Stewart of Ardshiel. Although the murderer was never caught or his identity established, James Stewart of the Glens was arbitrarily arrested and condemned by a jury packed with Campbells. Although the most important MacDonald families got off relatively lightly, one MacDonald estate was confiscated in its entirety, that of Keppoch, but it was recovered by clever legal argument before the Court of Session in 1755. Invergarry Castle, fortress of the MacDonnells of Glengarry, was slighted and torched, requiring the building of a new house, now the Glengarry Castle Hotel.

Invergarry Castle, seat of the MacDonnells of Glengarry – torched by Hanoverian forces after the Battle of Culloden.

For centuries, justice had been administered by the chief in consultation with appointed elders, whose opinion he would be expected to take into consideration. This ancient judicial prerogative of the chief was now taken over by a professional Scots Law judge, applying an entirely different legal philosophy. Scottish land law, based on feudal law, recognised only the rights of the chief as feudal superior of the clan lands – all others having inferior or no property rights. The chief landowner could dispense with both tacksman and the smaller tenants, and no longer measured his power in the number of armed men he could muster. In essence, much of the population was no longer needed by the chief. Populations in the Highlands and Islands were large compared with today, and some people began to leave.

Other punitive measures included the proscription of

Flora MacDonald (by Richard Wilson) (SNPG).

Highland dress, issued in the Unclothing Act of 1746, covering the wearing of tartan and plaid, and making the wearing of trousers compulsory. The playing of bagpipes was also banned. The Act threatened anyone wearing Highland dress with imprisonment for a first offence, and transportation for a second. The nobility and gentry defied the law with impunity. Flora was painted wearing a Royal Stewart tartan dress by Henry Raeburn, the famous Scottish portrait painter, in 1749, and was also shown with tartan in the portrait by Allan Ramsay. The young MacDonalds of Sleat were painted wearing tartan in 1750. Although the Act was repealed in 1783, few Highlanders went back to wearing their traditional garb. Many of the tartans to emerge after this time were based upon the once despised Government tartan, commonly known as the Black Watch tartan; others used the brighter industrial dyes, which also provided a greater range of colours and hues, rather than the original natural dyes. The famous painting of the Battle of Culloden by David Morier, an artist renowned for his accuracy, displayed many tartans which no longer exist.

The onslaught was extended to Gaelic culture and language, which was treated as inferior and essentially backward. In the new Scottish Sheriff Court in Skye, all cases were pleaded in English, a language unfamiliar to many on the island. Gaelic had long been seen by the Presbyterian Church of Scotland as a barrier to its spreading: it had been unable to penetrate far into the Highlands where Catholicism and Episcopalianism prevailed. Presbyterianism only succeeded when it accepted Gaelic as the language of evangelism, adopting the Gaelic Bible under pressure from Dr Samuel Johnson. Episcopalianism gradually adapted to the fact that Stewarts would not rule again: Charles and the Stewarts were eventually dropped from prayers.

7 – Flora's wedding

On 6 November 1750 Flora married Allan MacDonald, son of Alexander MacDonald of Kingsburgh, at Armadale. Allan was a lieutenant in Kirkibost's unit, which was based at Fort Augustus during the search for Prince Charles. Allan was reported as handsome with an athletic build, and had been educated at Edinburgh High School. Once he completed his education, he assisted his father's duties as the chamberlain to MacDonald of Sleat.

The marriage, as was then the custom on Skye, would have been preceded by a two-stage betrothal: the first very similar to the modern engagement, the second in which the dowry was finalised. A verbal contract was agreed before the wedding, but was signed on 3 December 1750, one month after the wedding, because the terms had to be reduced to proper legal form by two advocates in Edinburgh, presumably one representing each party. Rather than a prenuptial agreement, the contract was more a mutually agreed will, determining the disposal of the family estate in the event of the death of either or both the spouses.

Wedlock in Flora's day was more than a marriage of two individuals: it was in effect the marriage of two families. Flora's party to the contract was herself and her brother, now head of the MacDonalds of Milton, whereas Allan's party was himself and Alexander his father, obviously still head of the MacDonalds of Kingsburgh. The witnesses were Hugh MacDonald (Flora's stepfather), MacDonald of Castleton and Dr MacLean. The eldest son was to receive a better settlement than the younger, and boys were to receive more than girls. The latter could be explained in that the education of boys was more expensive than that of girls, because the boys had to go school in the Lowlands. The contract was five pages long and dealt exhaustively with different settlements for all eventualities.

Flora was styled as Flory throughout the document. This could not have been an error by the Edinburgh advocates because their draft had been rewritten by Dr MacLean on sheets of officially stamped paper. Although Allan may have used Flory as a term of endearment, its use in a legal document merits closer examination. It is possible that since she was now married into the MacDonalds of Kingsburgh, it was used out of deference to her mother-in-law: the Kingsburgh matriarch was also called Flora.

On the day of the wedding the groom and the bride were first entertained separately by their own family and friends, both parties coming together for the marriage ceremony. There is some disagreement over the dress that Flora wore, although some say it was the Stewart tartan dress painted by Raeburn and given to Flora by Lady Primrose on the condition that she wore it at her wedding – the family, however, have a dress of black silk, which they claim was the wedding dress. The new bride, on her first morning, would be dressed by her bridesmaids, wearing the cap of a married woman placed on her head by her mother. The bride would lead them out of the bridal chamber. The first male they encountered was obliged to address the bride with the 'Poet's Blessing', a poem he had written especially for her. The 'poet' was usually a relative of the groom.

The accommodation on Skye, even for the gentry, was typically a single-storey house with a thatched roof. There were only three houses with slate roofs in the whole of Skye: Monkstadt, Armadale and Dunvegan. The newest of these was Monkstadt, which was also the first to be roofed with slate. Most houses would have had floors of beaten earth, which would turn into mud if the house became flooded – this was experienced by Johnson and Boswell during their visit to Skye in 1773. Nevertheless, the homes would have been comfortably furnished in comparison to the simple houses of their tenants.

Although Skye had several castles, one-time impregnable fortresses, the advances in ordinance had rendered them obsolete as strongholds, and many were simply inconvenient and uncomfortable as residences. Most were abandoned, with the exception on Skye of Dunvegan, home of the MacLeods, which was sufficiently large and sheltered to be converted into a mansion. The original castle of the MacDonalds in the north of Skye was Duntulm, above cliffs but on a narrow and inaccessible site. Sir Alexander had abandoned this ancient castle in 1736, once his new house at Monkstadt was ready. This was part of a trend all over Scotland. The 3rd Duke of Argyll razed the old town and castle of Inveraray to the ground, and raised up the more gracious castle which exists today. Inveraray Castle was completed by Major General John Campbell of Mamore, when he became the 4th Duke of Argyll.

The castle of Duntulm quickly deteriorated in winter storms

Duntulm Castle – now a fragmentary ruin, on a strong cliff-top site. It was abandoned for Monkstadt House, itself now a ruin.

and, although it existed for centuries, little more survives than a few ruined walls. Monkstadt is also roofless and ruinous. The present Armadale Castle in Sleat, although also largely roofless and ruinous, post dates 1746. The Armadale house of Flora's day was by the shore next to the present youth hostel.

Food, based on dairy products, oatmeal and increasingly potatoes, would have been similar in all social strata. Meat would have been eaten infrequently, especially in the poorer households, where animal protein would have consisted of the innards of sheep, the basis of haggis, the world-renowned Scottish dish. While the poorer people would have drunk beer and whisky, their 'betters' had for centuries preferred imported wine and brandy.

Cattle or the bills of exchange, namely drovers' bills of sale, were often used to pay rents, instead of coin, which was in very short supply in Scotland. Even Dr Johnson had to trade a bill of exchange for coin from an English captain of a passing ship.

The black cattle had for centuries been a major source of income in Scotland. Although these beasts were smaller than their English counterparts, they were more hardy and could live off the very poor grazing which was common place in many parts of western Scotland. About the middle of the 18th century, the

English herd suffered from disease and this increased the demand for Scottish beef. The price of black cattle increased significantly over a very short period.

Cattle were driven from Skye through the narrow channel of sea between the island and the mainland at Kylerhea and Glenelg, which now has a car ferry during the summer months. From there, the cattle were led along the drover roads to the large cattle market at Crieff in Perthshire, and then to London and the south, many to be slaughtered in Smithfield, just outside the north wall of the City of London. Smithfield is also infamous in Scottish history as the place of execution of William Wallace.

In Flora's day many roads in Skye, as elsewhere in the Highlands, were drove roads for the annual cattle drive, and would have been unsuitable for carriages. The road that Flora rode upon on her way from Monkstadt to Kingsburgh was one of the first proper roads on Skye. These had been built by Sir Alexander in the previous decade. The main roads on Skye today are modern. Part of the original road survives at Armadale and has been incorporated into the gardens. Those who wish to walk in Flora's footsteps can do so.

When Sir Alexander had died on 23 November 1746, his son and successor, Sir James, was only five years old. The traditional society on Skye was therefore blown away without even an enlightened chief to moderate the storm following Culloden. Almost immediately, Lady Margaret, Sir Alexander's widow, took their children to Edinburgh for their education. Although adored by her tenants, she never liked Skye and its remoteness from the bright lights of the Lowlands. Sir James was brought up and influenced by the Enlightenment, which established Edinburgh as one of the most brilliant cities in Europe. Like any young gentleman of this period, he completed his education, received at Eton and Oxford, by going on the Grand Tour of the great centres of culture and learning of Europe. Sir James was a very gifted young man, deeply interested in the Gaelic culture of his clansmen – but he was never in good health.

Sir James had progressive ideas and brought in new people to transform his lands. Unfortunately, one was Charles MacQueen, who, although appointed on sound references, embezzled the rents and fled to Antigua. Sir James's continued poor health forced him to travel back to Rome, where he died in 1766 at the age of only 25 years. After James's death, his younger brother Sir Alexander became chief, but he, an Eton- and St Andrews-educated Guards officer, was typical of the new breed of Highland landowners. Sir Alexander was Anglocentric, married to an English wife, a relative of Boswell. As a serving soldier, he did not visit Skye often. He was created Lord MacDonald in 1776, and introduced the gathering of kelp, used in the production of glass and soap, to Skye, because it produced a handsome profit.

One of the first steps in the break up and selling off of the great Skye estates occurred when the MacLeods sold most of the Waternish peninsula to the Nicolsons. The interesting aspect of this sale was that centuries earlier, the MacNeacails or Nicolsons, a clan of Norse origin, were major landowners. They held Waternish, as well as Harris and Assynt (on the mainland), only to lose them when a MacNeacail heiress married a MacLeod. From the union rose the MacLeods of Harris. The remnant of the MacNeacails was recognised in its possession of Scorrybreck by the Lords of the Isles, and retained its independence under its own chief MacNeacail of Scorrybreck, although the MacDonalds had overlordship of that part of Skye.

For the first months of their lives together, Flora and Allan lived at Kingsburgh House until 1751 when they obtained the tack of Flodigarry. Their first son Charles was born on 22 October 1751, and they had four more of their seven children at Flodigarry: Anne in 1754, Alexander in 1755, Ranald in 1756 and James in 1757. Flodigarry was on the east side of the Trotternish peninsula at the foot of the Quiraing, a spectacular rock formation, which should have sheltered their farm from the worst of the Atlantic storms.

In 1755 Alexander MacDonald of Kingsburgh, Allan's father, retired as Chamberlain on an annual pension of £50. Allan succeeded his father as factor of MacDonald of Sleat's Trotternish estate, but they did not move back to Kingsburgh House until Flora, Allan's mother, died in March 1759. Alexander, himself, lived until 1772, taking up the tack of Monkstadt. Allan, with government encouragement, introduced a number of improvements which were working elsewhere in Britain, such as longer or 21-year leases, English or Welsh sheep, winter rotation of crops, and new kinds of crops such as new varieties of potatoes. These improvements were not entirely successful. Trotternish in

Flora's Cottage – Flora and Allan moved to Flodigarry and five of the children were born here (Flodigarry Country House Hotel).

particular, and the Highlands in general, had poor soil and sometimes cruel weather, and there was also a doubting and intransigent population who were suspicious of change. Flora had another child, John, in October of 1759.

Flora and Allan were not particularly liked on Skye, and many still thought she had done rather well out of her encounter with Bonnie Prince Charlie. The couple's progressive Lowland or English ideas, and even Flora's Lowland accent (which surprised many who met her) may have alienated folk on Skye. Flora and Allan also had a number of influential enemies, in particular Lady Margaret, widow of Sir Alexander, and the Martin family. The latter resented the transfer of the Flodigarry tack from themselves to Allan in 1751. This enmity persisted, even after the tack was restored to the Martins in 1763. This was exacerbated by the death of one of the family in 1765 after Allan had bearhugged him in a wrestling match.

The price of cattle dropped greatly in 1765, causing Allan to run up significant debts. One of the gravest problems Flora and Allan had was the substantial increase in rents to such levels that they almost exceeded that which the land could produce. Alexander MacDonald of Kingsburgh, even when his pension was taken into account, had only £17 a year to support himself and his servant after paying his rent. This, and the MacQueen fraud, would explain Allan's lack of success in business. Nevertheless, worse was to follow. Allan lost his job as factor in 1766, which was given to Dr MacLean. Flora was now 44 years old, and this year she gave birth to a daughter Frances or Fanny.

The couple were only left with the tack for Kingsburgh, which Allan successfully retained in 1767, securing a new lease from the Edinburgh-based land agent of the MacDonald estates, although for a considerably increased rent.

Allan was now more than 50 years of age, but still possessed a 'graceful mien and manly looks' when Dr Johnson and Boswell visited them (in 1773). Allan wore plaid, which was still forbidden. Johnson also described Flora as 'A woman of middle stature, soft features, gentle manners and elegant presence'. The family were in financial straits at the time – Flora was reduced to approaching friends to assist her. When Charles, their eldest son, was commissioned into the East India Company, Lady Primrose bought his uniforms and passage to India. Ranald was promoted to lieutenant in the Royal Navy.

Then, on 13 February 1772, Alexander MacDonald of Kingsburgh, Allan's father, died, thus cutting the last tie that kept Flora and Allan on Skye.

They decided to emigrate to America.

8 – A dance called 'America'

The rapid changes in administration and law of the Highland communities would have been sufficient to cause the collapse of the clan system. This was hastened by the fall in price of the black cattle, and then the black spring of 1771 and the severe winter of 1771-2, which effectively destroyed the community. Flora and Allan's herd of more than 300 beasts was wiped out. Skye society had degenerated into acrimony: the landlord sued his tenants for non payment of rents, and the tenants counter-sued for oppression and breach of contract.

At last the attraction of America overcame the Gaels' attachment to the sometimes cruel bonds of their homeland. This spread like an infection, beginning first with a few families until it caused whole districts, and then almost the whole community of Skye, to move. A dance popular in Skye at the time was called 'America'. This dance began with just one couple dancing until finally the whole of the assembly would join in.

Many people, who had already left Skye, were gentry rather than the poorer tenants who constituted the vast majority. Reports began to circulate that living conditions were better in America, particularly in Carolina. According to records of the time, it seemed as if everyone was talking about emigrating. By 1773 all of the name of MacDonald, except for a few old men, had already left or were going.

After John had settled into the High School in Edinburgh, one of the best schools of its day which his brothers had already attended, Flora and Allan sold up in 1774 and sailed down to Campbeltown, and there took passage in the *Wilmington* for Carolina. The ships of the time were frequently of dubious seaworthiness. Flora and Allan had a cramped cabin, but this would have been palatial in comparison to their erstwhile tenants, who lived in the squalor of the hold. The food and drinking water were appalling. It is not surprising that mortality on emigrant ships was high: virtually all infants and babies born onboard, and many of their mothers, died.

Flora's reputation had already preceded her to their plantation Mount Vernon in North Carolina, where she was welcomed and treated with great respect. Many of the old Skye tacksmen had already established themselves there, with some of the old tenants as indentured servants, thus preserving the culture and language of the old clan system, but in the New World.

For all its great natural beauty and bounty, the dense humid Carolina woodland might have appeared claustrophobic in contrast to their open, brisk and more barren sea-bound homeland.

Many of their fellow Caroliners were Scots, but a proportion of these were from the Lowlands or Scots-Irish, whose common language Scots was already contributing to the now characteristic dialect of the Southerner. In addition, their powerful Presbyterian view of the world contributed to their centuries-old distrust of the otherworldly Gael. This, in turn, reinforced the cohesion of the Gaelic settlers.

Even before Allan and Flora had arrived in 1774, the colonies were ablaze with dissatisfaction about rule from London. The surprising outcome was the support that the Gaels gave the Hanoverian government, when it would have been natural to have sided with the Patriots. Although there are a number of contributing reasons, the most important was that many influential Gaels, like Allan, were former Hanoverian officers, who would have sworn an Oath of Loyalty to George I and his heirs. Pressure would have been brought to bear on other Gaels, especially those who were newly arrived, and who looked to these influential men for leadership.

As the husband of the much-respected Flora, Allan was such a man of influence. Furthermore, as a former officer, he would have seen some of the atrocities perpetrated on Jacobite prisoners when he was stationed at Fort Augustus – he would not want to see that happen to his fellow Gaels again. The Governor of North Carolina, Martin (a Gaelic name), also had much influence over the Gaels.

The relationship between the colonies and the Hanoverian government in Britain broke down as London continued to assert its right to tax the colonists without giving them any direct representation. An attempt by a British unit to seize the arsenal at Concord led to a bloody confrontation – and the American War of Independence broke out in 1776. The Governor of North Carolina raised a regiment made up of Scottish Highlanders, the 34th Royal Highland Emigrant (North Carolina Regiment), in which both Allan and his two sons were enrolled, Allan as a Lieutenant Colonel. The regiment had representatives from many clans, including MacDonalds, MacLeods and Campbells.

As the conflict spread and deepened, the Patriots increased in number and strength, and became an effective fighting force, while Allan's regiment was the only Hanoverian unit in North Carolina. General MacDonald kept the Royal Highland regiment on the move, avoiding conflict until they could be reinforced. Unfortunately, the general fell ill, and was replaced by his second-in-command, Lieutenant Colonel MacLeod. Marching to the coast, where they could join Martin, the Governor, would have left their homes and families vulnerable to attack. MacLeod decided to attack while he still had some chance of winning.

A potential opportunity arose to confront the Patriots, who had a force similar in strength to the Royal Highland regiment and were based at Moores Creek.

MacLeod decided upon a surprise attack, but his intelligence was poor and they were not familiar with the forested territory, criss-crossed with rivers. The Highlanders advanced, but found themselves on the wrong side of the river. The only way to attack was across a wooden bridge, but the Patriots were forewarned and well prepared. The bridge had been weakened, reduced to its two main beams, and the entrenched Patriots had cannon loaded with grapeshot covering the approaches.

The Royal Highland regiment attacked across the remains of the bridge with drawn broadswords, only to be met by a storm of lead shot. Lieutenant Colonel MacLeod and Major Campbell fell almost immediately, the latter was shot over 20 times.

The badly mauled regiment, now led by Allan, attempted to retreat, but was intercepted 10 days later by a second Patriot force, and had to surrender. Although Allan, and one of his sons, Alexander, were captured, Captain MacLeod, his daughter Anne's husband, managed to escape.

In the aftermath of that defeat, the Patriots mercilessly hounded and harried all Highlanders. Flora was initially told that her husband Allan had been killed, and she became ill with a severe fever. Although she survived, her health suffered and she never properly recovered.

Flora was summoned before the Patriot Committee of Safety and charged with sedition. Although she put up a spirited defence, her lands, which she had held for just two years, were confiscated in 1777 and ravaged – Flora spent two further miserable years in hiding. Nevertheless, she rode on mercy missions, visiting and comforting friends who lost men. Many blamed Allan for persuading their men to join the Royal Highland regiment. During one of these missions, Flora fell and broke her arm. It was not properly set, and was to cause her problems for the rest of her life.

Allan petitioned congress repeatedly to be released, along with his son, by prisoner exchange. After 18 months, they finally relented, and allowed him to negotiate a suitable exchange with the Hanoverians in New York. Once released in August 1777, he was given the command of a company of New York Loyalists, and was directed to recruit Highlanders. Ranald, another of Flora and Allan's sons, was wounded at the Battle of Bunkers Hill.

Allan obtained a permit for Flora to leave North Carolina, which was now entirely in the hands of the Patriots. Flora left Mount Vernon after selling what she could, and took passage for New York. From there, the couple moved to Nova Scotia, where Allan served in the army for five further years. But, after only staying with him for one year, Allan recommended that Flora should return to Britain. Her health was failing, and she could not cope with the bitter winters.

9 – Back to Skye

Flora took passage back to Britain, but her ship was attacked by a French privateer. Instead of taking shelter below decks with the other ladies, Flora stayed on deck, encouraging the sailors to repel the privateer. During the action, she fell and broke her other arm. A medical student attended to her, but could not set her arm properly.

Her arrival in London in late 1779 was entirely different from her earlier visits, when she was the feted heroine, the saviour of Bonnie Prince Charlie. This time she was alone, mostly unknown, and deprived of the belongings that she had taken to America (some of which have since been donated to museums).

Upon hearing that her son Alexander was dead, drowned when his ship was lost returning to Britain, Flora's health failed. She was bedridden for nearly six months, during which time she was cared for by Dr Munro, a member of the important Edinburgh medical dynasty, whose mother was a Sleat MacDonald. Although Lady Margaret MacDonald of Sleat, now a dowager, was living in London at the time, there was no reconciliation between her and Flora.

Flora first returned to Edinburgh, staying with her old friend

Dunvegan Castle – when Flora returned from America she had no home, and she stayed at the castle with her daughter Anne.

and the now retired lawyer and Sleat land agent Mackenzie, and then in 1780 continued her convalescence on Skye, only to be informed that her son Ranald had also been lost at sea.

For five years, she had no permanent home, and instead stayed with friends and family in Skye and Uist. Flora lived on South Uist with her brother, presumably at Milton. She resided also at Dunvegan Castle for some time, where her daughter Anne now lived as she was married to Captain Alexander MacLeod of Lochbay, tutor to the young chief of the MacLeods.

In 1783, Allan's regiment was disbanded, and Allan was granted 3000 acres of land in Nova Scotia, some of which he cleared and built a hut. It is particularly commendable that,

Relics of Flora, including her stays, pin-cushion, a lock of Bonnie Prince Charlie's hair, and a portrait of Flora, on display at Dunvegan Castle along with many other treasures.

following the bitter failure of Skye and North Carolina, he could contemplate starting again at the age of 60. But in order to develop the land, he needed money. Allan returned to Britain in 1784 and travelled to London to present a claim to compensate for his family's losses in America in the King's cause. This claim included the plantation in North Carolina, and his two sons who had died in royal service. Allan only received £440 as compensation for the many losses suffered, and for which he had claimed £1341. This was in line with the other miserly awards made to those who suffered for their loyalty to the Hanoverians.

The compensation was not sufficient to work his lands in Nova Scotia and, since he was also getting on in years, he let the claim go and in 1784 returned to Skye.

Flora and Allan lived with their daughter Anne at Dunvegan Castle until 1787. They acquired a house at Peinduin, near Kingsburgh; Kingsburgh itself was leased to Captain MacDonald of Cuidreach, who married Flora's half-sister Anabella. Anne and her husband took control of a tack in Waternish in Stein, when Major General MacLeod returned from service in the British army.

Flora was now in poor health. She was crippled by rheumatism, and by her poorly set broken arms. She could do no more than sign letters which she had dictated.

On 4 March 1790 Flora died peacefully at Peinduin, in the presence of Allan and their children Charles, James, Anne and Fanny, and attended to by Dr John MacLean – only John was absent in India. It is reputed that Flora died in the bed that had been used by Bonnie Prince Charlie.

Flora's funeral was a touching affair. Her coffin was attended by a huge train of mourners and pipers from both of Skye's celebrated piping colleges, the MacCrimmons (MacLeod) and the MacArthurs (MacDonald), in addition to pipers from elsewhere. They all played the 'Coronach', the great lament of the Gael.

Flora was buried at Kilmuir cemetery with her husband's family, the MacDonalds of Kingsburgh. Allan eventually joined her, after his death on 20 September 1792.

In 1880 a large Celtic cross was erected as a memorial for her grave. Her best epithet came from Dr Johnson. Flora was 'a name that will be mentioned in history, and if courage and fidelity be virtues, mentioned with honour'.

Flora's grave and monument, Kilmuir burial ground.

10 – Epilogue

Flora's life spanned one of the most momentous periods in world history, a period which saw the collapse of the Jacobites and Stewart claim to the British throne and the American War of Independence and beginning of democracy and republicanism. Within a year of Flora's death, France, inspired by the success of the American Patriots, cut away its own monarchy and aristocracy upon the guillotine; republicanism European-style was born.

In the years following the 1745-6 Jacobite Rising, Flora's clan, in common with others, lost not only its clansmen and women, but also its lands. Flora's birthplace at Milton is a ruin, as is Monkstadt, while Nunton and Kingsburgh are in private hands. The Armadale Castle estate, and the seat of the Chiefs of MacDonald, is also now a ruin. It was bought back by Clan Donald worldwide, led by the MacDonald Steward Foundation in Canada and the American philanthropists Ellice McDonald CBE and Rosa Laird McDonald CBE, his wife. It was established as a home of Clan Donald by Trust Deed in 1972 as 'The Clan Donald Lands Trust'. The application of modern trust law has recreated the traditional concept of the clan's ownership of its lands. At the centre of these lands is the Flora MacDonald Suite.

Careers in the armed forces were considered the only respectable profession for the former MacDonald tacksmen, now that they were deprived of their lands and authority. As MacDonalds, it was their birth-right as descendants of Conn of the Hundred Battles and of the Norse kings. The British army and navy, East India Company, and the Dutch army now became the career destinations of the Protestant MacDonalds, including all of Flora's sons and most of her sons-in-law. Catholic MacDonalds were already long established in the Spanish and French armies. Neil MacDonald, upon his return to France and after he was sacked from Bonnie Prince Charlie's service, returned to French service when for a time the Prince became a Protestant. Neil is best remembered as being the father of the future Marshal of France, MacDonald, the Duke of Tarentum, one of Napoleon Bonaparte's longest serving generals. Opposing Napoleon at Waterloo was Colonel MacDonnell, brother of Glengarry, who commanding the Coldstream Guards, guarded the Duke of Wellington's right wing, repeatedly repelling a whole Corps.

Afterwards, the Duke pronounced him 'the bravest soldier in the British Army'.

In Scotland, the Gaelic culture with which Flora would have been familiar, did decline over the following years, and the Gaelic language has itself nearly become extinct and is still under threat. There has, however, been a revival with Gaelic-medium teaching in primary schools, even in Edinburgh, a resurgence of interest in Gaelic in the Lowlands, and the establishment of Sabhail Mòr Ostaig, a Gaelic college on Clan Donald land, now part of the University of the Highlands and Islands. This has been expanded to include Iomairt Cholm Cille, the Saint Columba Initiative, which, among others, aims to re-establish cultural and linguistic links between the Gaels in Scotland and Ireland, which Flora's clan, both as Lords of the Isles and after the Lordship's abolition, developed and maintained.

In 2000 the Gaelic-speaking members of the Scottish parliament debated in Gaelic, the first time the ancient tongue had been used in the parliament for nearly 700 years.

In America, where Flora was once despised and persecuted as an enemy, all was now forgiven. In death she had been able to conquer the hearts of her American foe as she had with her Hanoverian enemies. Flora's association with America has not been forgotten. Her estate is today called the Flora MacDonald Plantation, and there is also a Flora MacDonald Wing in the local Presbyterian seminary. Today, North Carolina is the home of a large Scottish-American community, with its thriving Gaelic culture and Highland games.

Flora has been revered by likening her to the great Biblical heroine, Ester, as the subject for a memorial window in St Columba's Episcopal Church in Portree. Ester saved her people from ruin, an event celebrated in the Jewish festival of Purim. The window was dedicated by Flora's great granddaughter, Fanny, in 1896. To say Flora had saved her people is surely too great a claim. She certainly protected her co-conspirators, who were largely MacDonald and MacLeod gentry, as they were able to shelter under her umbrella of public acclaim. It was beyond her power, however, to protect the ordinary clansmen and women, who suffered the full brunt of Hanoverian savagery. It is certainly true that Flora suffered grievously because of her sense of duty, first as a result of helping the Jacobite cause and Bonnie Prince

Charlie escape from Uist, then when supporting the Hanoverian government in the American War of Independence in North Carolina. It was a shame that duty and obligation often seemed only rewarded with betrayal and suffering.

The affection for Flora was not confined to her clan. One of the largest statues in Scotland, and certainly most prominently placed, is Flora's statue outside the west door of Inverness Castle. Her gaze is fixed upon the distant west, while at her side is a dog, representing fidelity.

Statue of Flora at Inverness Castle (Doug Houghton).

Map 3: Places of Interest

The notes below refer to the entries on the following pages:
Properties managed by Historic Scotland are indicated by (HS)
National Trust for Scotland are indicated by (NTS),
Normal admission prices: £ up to £2.50; ££ between £2.50
and £5.00; £££ more than £5.00. If there is any doubt about
access to sites, please check with the sites, check locally with
Tourist Information Centres, or check with land owners.
Confirm opening with sites before setting out.

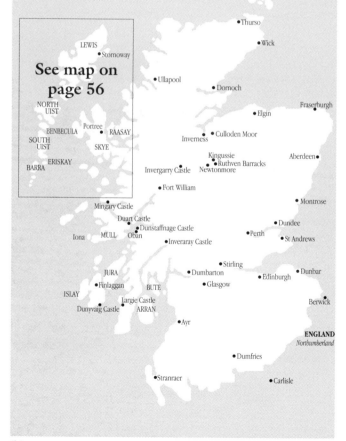

Places of Interest

Many places of interest are listed in this section, associated with Flora, the Jacobites and her clan the MacDonalds. Many can be visited and are established visitor attractions, but others are ruinous and should only be viewed from the exterior.

  Places associated with Flora include **Milton** on South Uist (her birthplace), and on Skye **Monkstadt House**, **Armadale** (where she was married), **Flodigarry** (where she gave birth to several of her children), **Dunvegan Castle** (where she lived for some time after returning from America – and has on display her stays, pin-cushion and portrait), **Peinduin** (where she died), and **Kilmuir** (where she is buried). Jacobite sites include **Bernera Barracks, Culloden Moor, Glenfinnan**, and **Ruthven Barracks**. Also included are several castles of the MacDonalds, such as **Armadale, Borve, Dun Sgathaich, Caisteal Camus, Duntulm, Dunyvaig, Finlaggan, Invergarry** and **Castle Tioram.**

Armadale Castle

Off A881, Armadale, SE of Sleat, Skye, Highland.
(NGR: NG 640047   LR: 32)
The present Armadale Castle was built in 1815 for the MacDonalds of Sleat after they had removed from Monkstadt, but there was an earlier house by the shore (near the youth hostel). Marion, Flora's mother was married to Hugh MacDonald of Armadale after her first husband, Ranald MacDonald of Milton, Flora's father, had died. Flora came to Armadale after helping Bonnie Prince Charlie escape to Skye in 1746, and was arrested and imprisoned some days later on her way to Castleton. Flora and Allan were later married here on 6 November 1750.

  The estate was sold, then was bought by Clan Donald worldwide, and established as a home of Clan Donald by Trust Deed in 1972 as 'The Clan Donald Lands Trust'.

  The main part of Armadale Castle, now ruined, has been

Map 4: Places of Interest:
Skye and the Western Isles

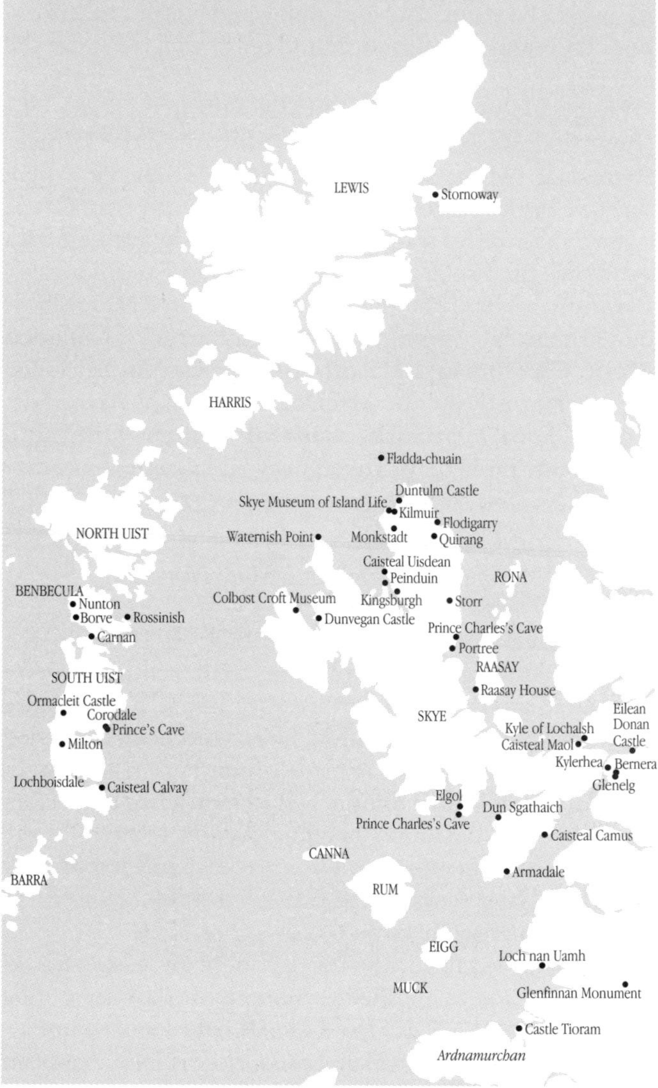

LEWIS

● Stornoway

HARRIS

● Fladda-chuain

Duntulm Castle

Skye Museum of Island Life ●
● Kilmuir

● Flodigarry

Waternish Point ● Monkstadt ● Quirang

Caisteal Uisdean
● Peinduin

RONA

NORTH UIST

BENBECULA

● Nunton
● Borve ● Rossinish
● Carnan

Colbost Croft Museum ● Kingsburgh ● Storr

● Dunvegan Castle

Prince Charles's Cave
● Portree

RAASAY

SOUTH UIST

● Raasay House

Ormacleit Castle
● Corodale
● Prince's Cave

SKYE

Eilean
Donan
Castle

● Milton

Kyle of Lochalsh
Caisteal Maol ●

Kylerhea ● Bernera

Lochboisdale ● Caisteal Calvay

Glenelg

Elgol
● Dun Sgathaich

Prince Charles's Cave
● Caisteal Camus

CANNA

BARRA

● Armadale

RUM

EIGG

Loch nan Uamh

MUCK

Glenfinnan Monument

● Castle Tioram

Ardnamurchan

landscaped and stands in 40 acres of fine woodland gardens and nature trails, as well as a walled kitchen garden. 'The Museum of the Isles', an exhibition covering 1300 years of the MacDonald clan and Lord of the Isles, opened in 2002. A library and study centre has facilities for genealogical research.

Self-catering accommodation is available to rent all year, and consists of seven cottages and the Flora MacDonald Suite.

Guided tours. Explanatory displays. Gift shops. Licensed restaurant. Tea room. Picnic area. WC. Disabled access. Car and coach parking. ££.

Open Apr-Oct, daily 9.30-17.30, last entry 17.00; gardens open all year; shop also open Nov-Mar, Mon-Fri 10.00-17.00.

Tel: 01471 844305/227   Fax: 01471 844275

Web: www.clandonald.com   Email: office@clandonald.com

Bernera Barracks

Off A87 at Shiel Bridge, 6 miles SE of Kyle of Lochalsh, 0.3 miles N of Glenelg, Bernera, Highland.
(NGR: NG 815197   LR: 33)

Built to control the crossing to Skye between Kylerhea and Glenelg, Bernera Barracks, dating from the 1720s, consists of ruined ranges of buildings around a courtyard, and had accommodation for over 200 men. The garrison was reduced after 1746, and the barracks were abandoned about 1800. The road to Glenelg mostly follows the course of an old military way and drove road from Skye to the south.

Borve Castle

Off B892, 3.5 miles S of Balivanich, Benbecula.
(NGR: NF 774506   LR: 22)

Only ruins remain of the castle. It was built by the MacDonalds, possibly by Amy MacRuari, first wife of John, Lord of the Isles, who was the progenitor of the Clanranald branch of the MacDonalds. It was occupied until at least 1625, around which time the family moved to Nunton. The castle was burned down in the late 18th century.

Caisteal Calvay

2 miles SE of Lochboisdale, N of Calvay, South Uist, Western Isles. (NGR: NF 817182   LR: 31)

Caisteal Calvay is a very ruined stronghold on a tidal islet to the north of the small island of Calvay in Loch Boisdale, and was formerly reached by a causeway. It was already ruinous when Bonnie Prince Charlie sheltered here in 1746. From Calvay, he was taken to Corodale and then Benbecula from where he was ferried across to Skye by Flora. Calvay can be seen from the ferry to Lochboisdale on South Uist.

Caisteal Camus

Off A851, 3.5 miles N of Armadale, Skye, Highland.
(NGR: NG 671087   LR: 32)

Standing in a picturesque location on a steep headland of the Sound of Sleat, Caisteal Camus – which is also known as Knock Castle – is a very ruinous stronghold of the MacLeods, then the MacDonalds of Sleat. It was abandoned about 1689.

Caisteal Maol

Off A850, 0.5 miles E of Kyleakin, Skye, Highland.
(NGR: NG 758264   LR: 33)

Overlooking the old ferry crossing and the new bridge between Skye and the mainland at Kyle of Lochalsh, Caisteal Maol, 'bare castle', is a very ruined keep, dating from the 15th century.

According to tradition, the castle was built by a Norse princess called 'Saucy Mary' who was married to a MacKin-non chief. Their main income was from tolls on ships sailing through the Kyle. It is said that she was buried beneath a large cairn [NG 602234] on the top of Beinn na Caillaich ('mountain of the old woman').

In the middle ages the castle was known as Dunakin, and a stronghold of the MacKinnons of Strath or Strathordil. The castle was probably abandoned some time around the middle of the 17th century when the MacKinnons moved to Kilmarie on the south of Skye.

The MacKinnons fought for the Marquis of Montrose at both Auldearn and Inverlochy in 1645, a MacKinnon regiment fought for Charles II at Worcester, and they were Jacobites, fighting at the Battle of Sheriffmuir in 1715 and Glenshiel in 1719. The Chief of MacKinnon sheltered Bonnie Prince Charlie in a cave near Elgol in 1746 when Charlie was a fugitive on Skye, for which he was given the recipe for Drambuie, a whisky liqueur, although the original recipe used cognac instead of whisky. **Access at all reasonable times.**

Caisteal Uisdein
Off A856, 3 miles S of Uig, Skye, Highland.
(NGR: NG 381583   LR: 23)
Caisteal Uisdean, 'Hugh's Castle', is a squat ruined rectangular 16th-century tower. Hugh MacDonald, the builder, was outlawed for piracy, his exploits extending even

to the fishermen of Fife, although he was later pardoned and made steward of Trotternish. He plotted to overthrow his MacDonald kin by slaughtering them at Castle Uisdean, however, but the plot was discovered, and he was eventually caught about 1602 and imprisoned in Duntulm Castle. He was given salted beef and no water, and when the pit where he had been buried was finally opened his corpse was found with a broken pewter jug, which he had destroyed with his teeth. His skull and thigh bones were kept in a window of the parish church, presumably at Kilmuir, until buried in 1827.

Castle Tioram

Off A861, 3 miles N of Acharacle, Moidart, Highland.
(NGR: NM 663725   LR: 40)
A substantial and picturesque ruin in a wonderful setting, Castle Tioram stands on a tidal island and was the seat of the MacDonalds of Clanranald. During the Jacobite Rising of 1715, the castle was torched so that Hanoverian forces could not use it, and the chief of Clanranald was killed at the Battle of Sheriffmuir. It was never reoccupied. Clanranald had a set of magic bagpipes which, when played, reputedly ensured victory in battle.
Care needs to be taken with tides.

Colbost Croft Museum

On B884, 4 miles NW of Dunvegan, Skye, Highland.
(NGR: NG 215485   LR: 23)
The museum is located in a blackhouse, and contains 19th-century implements and furniture, with a peat fire burning all day. There is a replica of an illicit whisky still.
Explanatory displays. Car and coach parking. £.
Open Easter-Oct, daily 9.30-18.00.
Tel: 01470 521296
Email: anniemac@annemacaskil.u-net.com

Colbost Croft Museum – see previous page.

Culloden Moor (NTS)

On B9006, 5 miles E of Inverness, Culloden, Highland.
(NGR: NH 745450   LR: 27)

It was here on the bleak moor of Drumossie that on 16 April 1746 the Jacobite army of Bonnie Prince Charlie was crushed by Hanoverian forces led by the Duke of Cumberland – the last major battle to be fought on British soil. The MacDonalds took their place on the left flank of the Jacobite army, but the Jacobites were tired and hungry. The Hanoverians had a better equipped and larger army: the battle turned into a rout and many Jacobites were slaughtered. Sites of interest include Old Leanach Cottage, Graves of the Clans, Wells of the Dead, Memorial Cairn, Cumberland Stone, and Field of the English.

Visitor centre with audiovisual programme. Bookshop.
Restaurant. WC. Disabled access to visitor centre, WC and
facilities. Car and coach parking. £.

Site open all year; visitor centre open daily: Feb-Mar & Nov-Dec, 11.00-16.00, closed 24-26 Dec; Apr-Jun & Sep-Oct, 9.00-18.00; Jul-Aug, 9.00-19.00.
Tel: 01463 790607   Fax: 01463 794294
Email: culloden@nts.org.uk

Duart Castle

Off A849, 2 miles S of Craignure, Duart, Mull, Argyll.
(NGR: NM 749354   LR: 49)

Built on a rocky knoll overlooking the Firth of Lorne and Sound of Mull, Duart is an extremely impressive and daunting fortress, dating from the 12th century.

The MacLeans of Duart claim descent from Gillean of the Battle Axe. Lachlan Lubanach married Lady Elizabeth, daughter of the Lord of the Isles, granddaughter of Robert II King of Scots, and was granted the first known charter for Duart, dated 1390, as her dowry. While fighting with the MacDonalds, the 6th chief Red Hector was killed at the Battle of Harlaw in 1411, slaying and being slain by Sir Alexander Irvine of Drum.

In 1674 the castle and lands were acquired by the Campbell Earl of Argyll. The MacLeans remained staunch supporters of the Stewarts throughout the Jacobite Risings.

The castle was not used as a residence, and was abandoned and became roofless after being garrisoned during the Jacobite Rising of 1745-6. It was acquired in 1911 by Fitzroy MacLean, 26th Chief, who restored the castle. *13th-century keep, exhibitions, dungeons and state rooms. Tea room and gift shop. WC. Picnic areas. Disabled access to tea room and gift shop. Car and coach parking. Group concessions. ££ (castle).*

Open Apr, Sun-Thu, daily 11.00-16.00; May-mid Oct, daily 10.30-18.00.

Tel: 01680 812309 Fax: 01680 812309
Web: www.duartcastle.com
Email: duartguide@isle-of-mull.demon.co.uk

Dun Sgathaich (Dunscaith)

Off A851, 6 miles NW of Armadale, Tokavaig, Skye, Highland. (NGR: NG 595121   LR: 32)

Standing on a rock, Dun Sgathaich is a small ruined 14th-century castle, probably incorporating an older castle or stronghold. Meaning 'Dun of the Shadow', Dun Sgathaich is associated with Diarmid, nephew of Finn MacCool. The warrior queen Sgathach trained men in the art of fighting, and Diarmid and Cuchullin came here to be instructed by her. Another tradition is that the castle was built in a single night by a witch.

Although the castle was originally held by the MacAskills, in the 14th century the lands of Sleat belonged to the MacLeods, and early in the 15th century passed to the MacDonalds. The castle was forfeited to the Crown around the 1490s with the destruction of the Lord of the Isles by James IV, but was besieged and captured by the MacLeods and MacLeans in support of the MacDonalds in 1515.

It was probably abandoned around 1618 when the MacDonalds of Sleat moved to Duntulm in Trotternish, although they later returned to Armadale in Sleat.

Dunstaffnage Castle (HS)

Off A85, 3.5 miles NE of Oban, Dunstaffnage, Argyll.
(NGR: NM 882344   LR: 49)

On a promontory in the Firth of Lorne, Dunstaffnage Castle is a massive ruinous courtyard castle, dating from the 13th century. A stronghold here was held by the kings of Dalriada in the 7th century, and was one of the places where the Stone of Destiny was kept. The present castle was built by the MacDougalls, but it was besieged and captured by Robert the Bruce in 1309. Bruce made the castle a royal property with the Campbells as keepers. In 1746 government troops occupied the castle during the Jacobite Risings, and Flora MacDonald was briefly imprisoned here in 1746. There is a fine ruined chapel nearby.

Gift shop. WC. Car and coach parking. £. Joint entry ticket available with Bonawe Iron Furnace.

Open Apr-Sep, daily 9.30-18.30; Oct-Mar, Sat-Wed 9.30-16.30, Thu 9.30-12.00, Sun 14.00-16.30, closed Fri; last ticket 30 mins before closing; closed 25-26 Dec.

Tel: 01631 562465

Duntulm Castle

Off A855, 6.5 miles N of Uig, Duntulm, Skye, Highland.
(NGR: NG 410743   LR: 23)

On a strong site above the sea and protected by cliffs, Duntulm Castle was once a strong and comfortable fortress and residence, but is now very ruinous. There was originally an Iron Age fortress here, later used by the Norsemen because of its strong position, then known as Dundavid or Dun Dhaibhidh. It was later a property of the MacLeods but was then held by the MacDonalds of Sleat, who made it their main seat. Hugh MacDonald (see also Caisteal Uisdein) was imprisoned and starved to death in a dungeon here after he had tried to seize the lands of Trotternish by murdering his kin. He was given only salted beef and no water. The castle was abandoned around 1730 when the Mac-Donalds moved to Monkstadt House.

Shulista was held by the MacLeans, hereditary physicians to the Mac-Donalds, while Hunglader was the home of their pipers, the Mac-Arthurs originally from Ulva, some of whom were buried at Kilmuir.

Parking Nearby.

View from exterior – care must be taken as dangerously ruined.

Dunvegan Castle

Off A850, 1 mile N of Dunvegan, Skye, Highland.
(NGR: NG 247491 LR: 23)

Standing on what was once an island, the castle has been continuously occupied by the chiefs of MacLeod since 1270, who trace their ancestry back to Leod, a son of Olaf the Black, Viking King of the Isle of Man. His stronghold was developed down the centuries into a large mansion and castle, and it is still owned by the 29th Chief of MacLeod.

Flora MacDonald stayed in the castle after returning here from North Carolina towards the end of her life. Her daughter Anne had married the tutor to the young chief of MacLeod. On display in the castle are Flora's stays, pin-cushion, and a lock of Bonnie Prince Charlie's hair, as well as a small portrait of Flora. Also on show are the spectacles of Donald MacLeod of Galtrigal and a glass given to him by Bonnie Prince Charlie. MacLeod was the pilot on the famous boat-trip across to Skye, and he was arrested and tried for treason.

Dunvegan is also the home to the famous Fairy Flag, 'Am Bratach Sith' in Gaelic. There are many legends surrounding this piece of silk, which is now reduced in size (from pieces being removed and kept for luck) and somewhat threadbare. One is that it was given to one of the chiefs by his fairy wife at their parting. This is said to have taken place at the Fairy Bridge, three miles to the north east, at a meeting of rivers and roads. The chief had married his wife thinking she was a mortal woman, but she was only permitted to stay with him for 20 years before returning to Fairyland. The flag, however, originates from the Middle East, and it has been dated between 400 and 700 AD, predating the castle by hundreds of years. The flag is believed to give victory to the clan whenever unfurled, and

was also believed to make the marriage of the MacLeods fruitful, when draped on the wedding bed, and to charm the herrings out of Dunvegan Loch when unfurled. Belief in its power was such that during World War II pilots from the clan carried a picture of the flag as a talisman.

Other fascinating items at Dunvegan include a drinking horn, 'Rory Mor's Horn', which holds several pints of claret, and the heir of the MacLeods had to empty in one go; and the Dunvegan Cup, gifted to the clan by the O'Neils of Ulster in 1596. The MacCrimmon Pipes, associated with MacCrimmons of Borreraig, who were hereditary pipers of the MacLeods, are also on display. There is also information about St Kilda, which was formerly a property of the family.

Boat trips can be taken from the castle to a nearby seal colony, where the seals can be seen at close hand.

Info cards in various languages in each of the public rooms. Guides on-hand. Audio-visual theatre. Gift shops. Restaurant. WC. Gardens. Boat trips (££) to seal colony. Dunvegan seal colony. Pedigree Highland cattle fold. Car and coach parking. Group/student/OAP concessions. Holiday cottages available, also wedding venue. £££.
Open all year: Mar-Oct, daily 10.00-17.30; Nov-Mar, daily 11.00-16.00; closed 25-26 and 1-2 Jan; last entry 30 mins before closing.
Tel: 01470 521206   Fax: 01470 521205
Web: www.dunvegancastle.com
Email: info@dunvegancastle.com

Dunyvaig Castle

Off A846, 2 miles E of Port Ellen, Lagavulin, Islay, Argyll. (NGR: NR 406455   LR: 60)
Little remains of the castle, except ruined walls on top of a rock by the sea and some remains of the courtyard. The castle belonged to the MacDonald Lord of the Isles, who had their main seat at Finlaggan, also on Islay. The Lord of

the Isles was forfeited by James IV in 1493, and the castle was fought over many times. The property passed to the Campbells of Cawdor, who held the castle until about 1677, but demolished it soon afterwards, and moved to Islay House. The castle stands on the shore near Lagavulin Distillery.

Parking nearby.

Access at all reasonable times – care should be taken.

Eilean Donan Castle

On A87, 8 miles E of Kyle of Lochalsh, Dornie, Highland. (NGR: NG 881259   LR: 33)

One of the most beautifully situated of all castles, Eilean Donan Castle is a grand fortress on a small island in a sea loch. It was a property of the Mackenzies, and Eilean Donan became their main stronghold. Robert the Bruce sheltered here in 1306.

In 1539 it was besieged by Donald Gorm MacDonald, a claimant to the Lordship of the Isles, but he was killed by an arrow shot from the castle. William Mackenzie, 5th Earl of Seaforth, had it garrisoned with Spanish troops during

the Jacobite rising of 1719, but three frigates battered it into submission with cannon, and it was blown up from within. The Battle of Glenshiel took place at the head of Loch Duich, near Shiel Bridge, and the site is marked by an information board. There are mementoes of Bonnie Prince Charlie and James VIII.

Visitor centre. Exhibitions. Gift shop. Tearoom. WC and disabled WC. Car and coach parking. ££.

Open mid Mar-3rd week Nov, daily 10.00-17.30, except until Easter and from Oct, daily 10.00-15.30.
Tel: 01599 555202   Fax: 01599 555262
Web: www.eileandonancastle.com
Email: info@donan.f9.co.uk

Finlaggan

Off A846, 3 miles W of Port Askaig, Loch Finlaggan, Islay, Argyll. (NGR: NR 388681   LR: 60)
Finlaggan was a very important site in medieval times, but not much remains except foundations on two islands. The ruins of a chapel, dedicated to St Finlaggan a contemporary

69

of St Columba, and many other buildings stand on the larger island, Eilean Mor. There are several carved gravestones, thought to commemorate relatives of the Lords of the Isles, who were themselves buried on Iona.

There was a kingdom of the Isles, subject to Norway, from about 900. In the 12th century, Somerled, of mixed Norse and Celtic blood, ousted the Norsemen from much of western Scotland and took control of their territories, although he remained the vassal of the King of Man. He was assassinated at Renfrew in 1164 when at war with Malcolm IV, King of Scots.

Somerled was succeeded by his sons Reginald in Kintyre and Islay; Dugald in Lorne, Mull and Jura; and Angus in Bute, Arran and North Argyll.

The whole area became part of the kingdom of Scots in 1266 after the Scots had defeated the Norwegians at the Battle of Largs three years earlier.

Angus Og MacDonald (Young Angus MacDonald) was the grandson of Donald, a son of Reginald: hence the name MacDonald or Clan Donald. Angus was a friend and supporter of Robert the Bruce, fought at Bannockburn, and died at Finlaggan in 1328: his son, John of Islay, was the first to use the title 'Lord of the Isles'.

The independence of the Lords, however, and their power and influence, caused constant trouble for the kings of Scots. A campaign by the 2nd Lord led to the bloody Battle of Harlaw in 1411, and the 3rd Lord was twice imprisoned by James I. In 1461 John, 4th Lord of the Isles and Earl of Ross, signed the Treaty of Westminster-Ardtornish by which he, the Earl of Douglas, and Edward IV of England agreed to divide Scotland between them.

James IV eventually destroyed the power of the Lords in a campaign in 1493, and had John, imprisoned at Paisley Abbey until his death in 1503. Attempts were made to restore the Lordship, but these were ultimately unsuccessful, although a branch of the MacDonalds held the lands until the beginning of the 17th century, when they passed to the Campbells. There is a visitor centre near the island.

Visitor centre. Parking nearby.

Open Apr-Oct: tel to confirm.

Tel: 01496 810629   Fax: 01496 810856

Web: www.islay.com   Email: lynmags@aol.com

Flodigarry

Off A855, 17 miles N of Portree, Flodigarry, Skye,
Highland. (NGR: NG 464719   LR: 23)

Located in a spectacular scenic location beneath the Quirang, Flora's Cottage at Flodigarry is where Flora and Allan stayed between 1751-2 and 1759 after they were married. They had acquired the tack from the Martin family, and five of their children were most likely born here: Charles, Anne, Alexander, Ranald and James.

The nearby house, which incorporates old work, was built in 1895 by Alexander Livingstone MacDonald, who is believed to have been a descendant of Flora. From 1928

Quirang – this dramatic area is near Flora's cottage at Flodigarry, which is now part of the Flodigarry County House Hotel.

the house has been used as the Flodigarry Country House Hotel. Flora's cottage now houses seven hotel bedrooms, each named after Flora's children. It is situated in the sheltered hotel grounds adjacent to the main house. Most rooms have lovely views over the cottage garden.

Hotel – open all year.
Tel: 01470 552203   Fax: 01470 552301
Web: www.flodigarry.co.uk   Email: info@flodigarry.co.uk

Flora MacDonald's Statue, Inverness Castle
Off A82, Castle Wynd, Inverness Castle, Inverness, Highland. (NGR: NH 666450 LR: 26).
This is one of the largest statues in Scotland, and is located outside the west door of Inverness Castle. Flora's gaze is fixed upon the distant west, while at her side is a dog, representing fidelity.

Inverness was strategically important and there was a strong castle here from early times. It was captured by the Jacobites during the 1745-6 Rising, but was destroyed following the Battle of Culloden. A mock castle replaced the old building, which was used as a court house.
Access to statue at all reasonable times.

Fort William
Off A82, 1.5 miles NE of Fort William, Inverlochy, Highland. (NGR: NN 104742 LR: 41)
Fort William is named after the now ruinous fort, which was built by General Monck for Cromwell during the 1650s, then reconstructed and renamed in 1690, during the reign of William of Orange. It was bombarded in the spring of 1746 by Jacobites, but could not be taken.

The fort was garrisoned until 1866, after which most of it was demolished, although remains of the ramparts and bastions as well as the sallyport survive. The West Highland Museum in the town has information about the fort.

Glenfinnan Monument (NTS)

On A830, 15 miles NW of Fort William, Glenfinnan, Highland. (NGR: NM 906805   LR: 41)

In the grand and scenic location at the head of Loch Shiel, it was here on 19 August 1745 that the standard was raised by the Jacobites under Bonnie Prince Charlie for James VIII and III, so beginning the 1745-6 Rising. The Glenfinnan Monument, in this picturesque setting, was built in 1815 to commemorate the many who fought and died for Bonnie Prince Charlie.

Visitor centre. Gift shop. Snack bar. WC. Disabled facilities. Parking. £.

Site open all year; visitor centre, shop and snack bar open Apr-Jun & Sep-Oct, daily 10.00-17.00; Jul-Aug 9.30-17.30.

Tel/fax: 01397 722250   Email: glenfinnan@nts.org.uk

Highland Folk Museum, Kingussie

Off A9, 12 miles SW of Aviemore, Duke Street, Kingussie, Strathspey, Highland. (NGR: NH 758007   LR: 35)

The museum features collections devoted to Highland social history, displayed in realistic settings and reconstructed buildings. There is a Lewis blackhouse and a clack mill. Displays include farm machinery, country crafts, domestic life, costume and furniture.

Gift shop. Picnic area. WC. Disabled access. Car and coach parking. £.

Open Apr-Oct: Apr-Sep, Mon-Sat 9.30-17.30; Oct, Mon-Fri 9.30-16.30.

Highland Folk Museum, Newtonmore

Off A9, Autlarie, Newtonmore, Highland.
(NGR: NN 700980   LR: 42)

A fascinating glimpse into 300 years of Highland life with a reconstructed 18th-century township with costumed interpreters. There is also an early 20th-century school and

clockmakers shop, and a working croft.
Gift shop. WC. Disabled access to ground floor. Parking. £.
Open Apr-Aug, daily 10.30-17.30; Sep, daily 11.00-16.30; Oct, Mon-Fri 11.00-14.30.

Tel: 01540 661307   Fax: 01540 661631
Web: www.highlandfolk.com
Email: highland.folk@highland.gov.uk

Inveraray Castle

Off A83, N of Inveraray, Argyll.
(NGR: NN 096093   LR: 56)
Inveraray Castle, a large mansion with towers and turrets, was begun in 1744 for the Campbell Dukes of Argyll. It

was remodelled by William and John Adam, and then again in 1877 after a fire. Major General John Campbell of Mamore became the 4th Duke of Argyll, and the castle is still the seat of the Dukes of Argyll. The Clan Room features information of special interest to members of Clan Campbell.
Guided tours. Collections of tapestries and paintings.

*Displays of weapons. Rob Roy MacGregor's sporran and
dirk handle. Clan Room. Gift shop. Tea room. WC. Picnic
area. Woodland walks. Disabled access to ground floor only.
Car and coach parking. £££.*
Open 3rd Apr-Oct (2004): tel to confirm.
Tel: 01499 302203   Fax: 01499 302421
Web: www.inveraray-castle.com
Email: enquiries@inveraray-castle.com

Invergarry Castle

*Off A82, 7 miles SW of Fort Augustus, Highlands.
(NGR: NH 315006   LR: 34)*
Invergarry Castle is a very impressive ruin, dating from the
17th-century. The fortress stands on the 'Rock of the
Raven', the slogan of the family. The castle was built by
the MacDonnells of Glengarry, and was twice visited by
Bonnie Prince Charlie during the Jacobite Rising of
1745-6. Afterwards it was burnt by the 'Butcher' Duke of
Cumberland. Colonel MacDonnell, brother of Glengarry,
commanded the Coldstream Guards and guarded the Duke
of Wellington's right wing at Waterloo. The Duke
pronounced him 'the bravest soldier in the British Army'.
A new mansion had been built nearby the ruined castle, on
the site of which is the Glengarry Castle Hotel.
Parking nearby.
**Glengarry Castle Hotel – open 19 Mar-15 Nov
2004. Ruin can be seen from grounds of hotel – the
interior of the old castle is in a dangerous condition.**
Tel: 01809 501254   Fax: 01809 501207
Web: www.glengarry.net   Email: castle@glengarry.net

Kilmuir

*Off A855, 4 miles N of Uig, Kilmuir, Skye, Highland.
(NGR: NG 399719   LR: 23)*
In Flora's day Kilmuir was the site of the parish church,
dedicated to St Mary, but nothing remains of this church
[NG 400717] except its burial ground. The MacDonalds

were buried here, as were the MacArthurs of Ulva, their pipers, and there are some interesting memorials. A Celtic cross marks the burial place of Flora MacDonald. Allan, her husband, and others of her family were also laid to rest here. The burial ground is near the Skye Museum of Island Life.

Access at all reasonable times.

Kingsburgh House

Off A856, 5 miles S of Uig, Kingsburgh, Skye, Highland. (NGR: NG 393554   LR: 23)

Kingsburgh, or Kysburg, is mentioned in 1557, and was a property of the MacDonalds. Bonnie Prince Charlie was brought here in 1746 while a fugitive from Hanoverian forces. This was the home of Alexander MacDonald of Kingsburgh, factor of the MacDonalds of Sleat. Allan MacDonald of Kingsburgh married Flora MacDonald at Armadale. The existing house may incorporate an older building dating from the 18th century.

Private House – not open to the public.

Largie Castle

Off A83, 17 miles SW of Tarbert, Argyll. (NGR: NR 708483   LR: 62)

Site of castle, little of which survives. The property was held by the MacDonalds of Largie from the middle of the 15th century until the 20th century. The family moved to 'new' Largie Castle, 0.5 miles north-east of Tayinloan. Flora visited her MacDonald relatives at Largie.

Loch nam Uamh Cairn

Off A830, 8 miles S of Mallaig, Cuildarrach, Loch nan Uamh, Highland. (NGR: NM 720844   LR: 40)

It was from here that Bonnie Prince Charlie sailed for France, never to return, on 20 September 1746.

Car parking.

Access at all reasonable times.

MacNab's Inn (Royal Hotel), Portree

Off A855, Skye, Highland. (NGR: NG 483435   LR: 23)
Bonnie Prince Charlie visited MacNab's Inn (for many years the only public house on the island) in Portree in 1746, and it was here he parted from Flora. The Royal Hotel stands on the site, overlooking the picturesque harbour of Portree, and has been owned by the MacLeod family for more than 50 years. MacNab's Cask Conditioned Ale, which is brewed by the Isle of Skye Brewing Company at Uig, is exclusive to the hotel bars.
Family-run hotel with 21 rooms, Well Plaid restaurant, bar and diner, fitness centre and sauna.
Tel: 01478 612525   Fax: 01478 613198
Web: www.royal-hotel-skye.com
Email: info@royal-hotel-skye.com

Milton

Off A865, 6 miles NW of Lochboisdale, Milton, South Uist, Western Isles. (NGR: NF 741269   LR: 22)
The remains of the ruined cottage, one wall of which remains, where Flora MacDonald was born in 1722. Flora may have also stayed here with her brother on her return from North Carolina. There is a memorial cairn and plaque.
Access at all reasonable times.

Mingary Castle

Off B8007, 1 mile E of Kilchoan, S coast of Ardnamurchan, Highland. (NGR: NM 502631   LR: 47)
Mingary is a strong courtyard castle encircling the rock on which it stands, dating from the 13th century. It was probably built by the MacIains of Ardnamurchan.

   The MacIains supported the MacDonalds in the 1550s, and MacLean of Duart captured the chief of MacIain, then unsuccessfully besieged the castle with Spanish soldiers from an Armada galleon in Tobermory Bay. The Campbells, however, took Mingary from the MacIans.

The castle was garrisoned for the Government during the Jacobite Rising of 1745-6, and was probably still habitable around 1848. The castle can be reached from along the shore from Kilchoan pier.

View from exterior.

Monkstadt House

Off A855, 2 miles N of Uig, Linicro, Monkstadt, Trotter-nish, Skye, Highland. (NGR: NG 380676   LR: 23)

The ruinous house, dating from around 1732, replaced a dower house of the second half of the 17th century, built for the widow of John Mor MacDonald.

It was rebuilt by Sir Alexander MacDonald of Sleat as a replacement for nearby Duntulm Castle, which stands in a windswept and inaccessible site.

Bonnie Prince Charlie, disguised as Betty Burke, was brought to Skye from Rossinish on Benbecula in 1746 by

Flora MacDonald. He was being hunted by Hanoverian forces, and when Flora arrived at Monkstadt it was soon clear that it was not safe. The Prince was taken south, straight to Kingsburgh House and he never came to Monkstadt.

The MacDonalds of Sleat left in 1798, and Monkstadt was used by tacksmen who held the nearby lands. The house was ruinous by the middle of the 20th century, but is still an interesting pile.

View from exterior.

Ormacleit Castle

Off A865, 9.5 miles N of Lochboisdale, Ormacleit, South Uist, Western Isles. (NGR: NF 740319 LR: 22)

One of the last castles built in Scotland, Ormacleit was built as the residence of Ailean, Chief of Clanranald, at the beginning of the 18th century. It was accidentally destroyed by fire in 1715, on the eve of the Battle of Sheriffmuir during the Jacobite Rising, when the Clanranald chief was killed. It was never rebuilt, although part has recently been reoccupied.

View from exterior.

Peinduin

Off A856, 3.5 miles S of Uig, 1 mile N of Kingsburgh,
Skye, Highland. (NGR: NG 385575   LR: 23)

The abandoned and ruinous township, north of the River
Hinnisdal, is where Flora MacDonald died in 1790 at the
age of 67 years old. She probably had lived in the now
ruinous two-storey building, and was attended by Allan
her husband and children at her bedside. Indeed, it is said
that the bed in which she died was that which Bonnie Prince
Charlie had slept in at Kingsburgh.

  She was buried at Kilmuir.

Prince Charles's Cave, Elgol

Off A881, 1 mile S of Elgol, Prince Charles's Cave, Skye,
Highland. (NGR: NG 517124   LR: 23)

The cave is where Bonnie Prince Charlie was sheltered by
the MacKinnons while a fugitive on the island in 1746. It
is in a remote spot by the sea.

Cuillin Mountains from Elgol.

Prince Charles's Cave, Portree

Off A855, 3.5 miles NE of Portree, Skye, Highland.
(NGR: NG 518482   LR: 23)
In a remote location below cliffs is the cave where Bonnie
Prince Charlie is said to have sheltered before being taken
across to Raasay.

Prince's Cave, Glen Corodale

Off A865, 9 miles N of Lochboisdale, Glen Corodale, South
Uist, Western Isles. (NGR: NF 833313   LR: 22)
The small cave was used to shelter the Prince when he was
on South Uist. It is in a very remote spot on the east coast
of the island.

Quirang

Off A855, unclassified Staffin to Uig road, 19 miles N of
Portree, Quirang, Skye, Highland.
(NGR: NG 455695   LR: 23)
An impressive group of towers and pinnacles, reached by a
rough track (which is not suitable for the elderly and infirm).
The Needle is an obelisk some 120 feet high, and the Table
stands in a large natural amphitheatre. Flodigarry is near
here.
Limited car parking.
Access at all reasonable times.

Raasay House

Off minor road, 2 miles N of East Suinish pier, Clachan,
Raasay, Highland.
(NGR: NG 546366   LR: 32)
Near the present house is the site of a 16th-century tower
house, known as Kilmaluag Castle because of the proximity
of St Moluag's church.
   The main residence of the MacLeods of Raasay had been
at Brochel Castle, but they moved here in the 17th century.

The tower of Kilmaluag, or a later residence, was torched after the Jacobite Rising, and replaced in 1747 by the present Raasay House, built by the 10th chief – Bonnie Prince Charlie was briefly sheltered on Raasay in 1746. The last traces of the castle were removed in 1846, and it was in this year that the 12th and last chief of MacLeod had to sell the property.

Raasay House has multi-activity holidays and day activities, including courses in windsurfing, sailing, and kayaking as well as rock climbing, abseiling, archery and orienteering. Local information on the surrounding sites of interest, as well as historic and natural beauty spots, is also available. A heritage museum (tel: 01478 660207) is located in the west wing, and has displays of artefacts from Raasay.

Outdoor sports tuition. Gift shop. Restaurant and cafe. Garden. WC. Disabled access. Car and coach parking. Accommodation.

Open Mar-Oct: tel to confirm.

Tel: 01478 660266   Fax: 01478 660200

Web: www.raasay-house.co.uk

Email: info@raasay-house.co.uk

Ruthven Barracks (HS)

Off A9, 1 mile S of Kingussie, Ruthven Barracks, Highland. (NGR: NN 764997   LR: 35)

Nothing remains, except substantial earthworks, of a 13th-century stronghold. In 1718 the castle was demolished and replaced by a barracks for Hanoverian troops. It was held by government forces in 1746, but was eventually burnt by Jacobite forces who had gathered here after the Battle of Culloden in 1746. Word soon came through that Bonnie Prince Charlie had fled. The barracks were not restored, and the buildings are ruinous.

Car parking.

Access at all reasonable times.

Tel: 01667 460232

Ruthven Barracks, Kingussie (Doug Houghton).

Skye Museum of Island Life, Kilmuir

On A855, 5 miles N of Uig, Skye, Highland.
(NGR: NG 394717 LR: 23)
The museum illustrates the life of a crofting community
from around the turn of the 19th century, and is housed in
a group of seven thatched buildings, including a blackhouse
and smithy. Displays include a wide range of agricultural
implements and a house with period furniture. Flora is
buried in the nearby churchyard at Kilmuir, her grave
marked by a Celtic cross.
Explanatory displays. Gift shop. WC. Car and coach
parking. Group concessions. £.
Open Easter-Oct, Mon-Sat 9.30-17.30.
Tel: 01470 552206   Fax: 01470 552206

St Columba's Episcopalian Church, Portree

Somerled Square, Skye, Highland. (NGR: NG 483435 LR: 23)
The church has a fine stained glass window which
commemorates Flora MacDonald. The window was
dedicated by Flora's great granddaughter, Fanny, in 1896.

Skye Museum of Island Life, Kilmuir – see previous page.

Storr

Off A855, 7 miles N of Portree, Storr, Skye, Highland.
(NGR: NG 498541   LR: 23)
A collection of pinnacles, rock formations and crags, rising
to some 2360 feet. The Old Man of Storr, at the east side
of the Storr, is a black pinnacle, 160 feet high. Due to
erosion Storr is now closed to walkers although it can be
viewed from the main road.
Car parking.
Open all year to view.

West Highland Museum, Fort William

Off A82, Cameron Square, Fort William, Highland.
(NGR: NN 102738   LR: 41)
The museum features displays on traditional Highland life
and culture. There are many Jacobite mementoes.
Guided tours. Explanatory displays. Gift shop. WC.
Disabled access. Car parking nearby (£ May-Oct). £.
Open: Jun-Sep, Mon-Sat 10.00-17.00; Jul-Aug, also
Sun 14.00-17.00; Oct-May, Mon-Sat 10.00-16.00.
Tel: 01397 702169   Fax: 01397 701927
Web: www.westhighlandmuseum.org.uk
Email: info@westhighlandmuseum.org.uk

Index

Underlined page numbers refer to an illustration
Page numbers in **bold** refer to the main entry in the places of interest